How to
Select and Renovate
an
Older House

—◆—

Gerald E. Sherwood

DOVER PUBLICATIONS, INC.
New York

PREFACE

The wood-frame house has been one of the most prevalent forms of shelter in the United States since the days of the early settlers. As a result, there are houses of various ages in outmoded and deteriorating condition in almost every community across the country. Some are being razed while others are simply abandoned. In either case they must be replaced by a new living unit at a high cost and with the consequent drain on our natural resources. Many of these homes could be rehabilitated at a lower cost than that of new construction and with desirable material savings. This handbook was developed to promote the twofold advantage of lower cost housing and conservation of our natural resources.

The principles spelled out here can likewise be used for more minor renovations of the home.

The appraisal section is a guide for appraising the suitability of wood-frame dwellings for rehabilitation. A systematic approach for inspecting the building and evaluating information from the inspection is presented.

If the building is determined to be worthy, the rehabilitation portion is a guide for planning and accomplishing the rehabilitation of a building that has been found suitable. Detailed instructions, including numerous illustrations, are presented.

This handbook should be particularly useful to homeowners and prospective buyers of older homes. It should also be of interest to carpenters, contractors, and lending institutions, and various groups that seek to maintain and improve homes within a community.

CONTENTS

Page

APPRAISAL _____ 1
Introduction _____ 1
Masonry and Concrete _____ 1
  Foundations _____ 1
  Masonry Veneers _____ 3
  Chimneys and Fireplaces _____ 3
Structural Wood Frame _____ 4
  Floor Supports _____ 4
  Floor Framing _____ 4
  Wall Framing _____ 4
  Roof Framing _____ 4
Exterior _____ 4
  Siding and Trim _____ 4
  Windows _____ 5
  Doors _____ 5
  Porches _____ 5
  Finishes _____ 5
  Roof _____ 6
Interior _____ 6
  Flooring _____ 6
  Walls and Ceilings _____ 6
  Trim, Cabinets, and Doors _____ 7
Recognizing Damage by Decay and Insects _____ 7
  Decay _____ 7
  Insect Problems _____ 9
Insulation and Control of Moisture _____ 9
  Insulation _____ 10
  Vapor Barriers _____ 10
  Ventilation _____ 10
Mechanical _____ 10
  Plumbing _____ 10
  Heating _____ 11
  Electrical _____ 12

Page

General Considerations _____ 12
  Circulation _____ 12
  Layout _____ 12
  Appearance _____ 13
Final Evaluation _____ 14
  Major Reasons for Rejection _____ 14
  Guideposts for the Final Decision _____ 14
  Cautions _____ 14
REHABILITATION _____ 16
Introduction _____ 16
Developing the Plan _____ 16
  General Layout _____ 16
  Expansion Within the House _____ 19
  Additions _____ 21
  Remodeling the Kitchen _____ 22
  Adding a Bath _____ 23
  Appearance _____ 24
Reconditioning Details _____ 26
  Basic Structure _____ 26
  Openings _____ 47
  Insulation and Moisture Control _____ 54
  Interior Items _____ 59
  Specific Features _____ 69
  Additional Space _____ 73
  Painting and Finishing _____ 79

SUMMARY _____ 83

APPENDIX _____ 84
  Terminology _____ *inside back cover*
  Glossary of Housing Terms _____ 84
  Index _____ 90

Published in Canada by General Publishing Company, Ltd., 30 Lesmill Road, Don Mills, Toronto, Ontario. Published in the United Kingdom by Constable and Company, Ltd., 10 Orange Street, London WC2H 7EG.

This Dover edition, first published in 1976, is a republication of Agriculture Handbook No. 481, *New Life for Old Dwellings: Appraisal and Rehabilitation,* prepared by the Forest Service of the United States Department of Agriculture, 1975.

International Standard Book Number: 0-486-23374-X
Library of Congress Catalog Card Number: 76-9184

Manufactured in the United States of America
Dover Publications, Inc.
180 Varick Street
New York, N.Y. 10014

APPRAISAL

INTRODUCTION

The wood frame house has been one of the most prevalent forms of shelter in the United States since the days of the early settlers in the 17th century. As a result, there are houses of various ages in almost every community across the country. Some have been well maintained and remodeled to keep pace with contemporary living requirements; but a large percentage of older houses are lacking in modern conveniences and comforts. Through neglect, many such houses are in a deteriorating or dilapidated condition.

Unlike most material objects, a well-built house properly maintained does not wear out—at least not over a period of several hundred years. It may become outdated and lack certain conveniences and comforts, but it does not wear out. Tests conducted by the Forest Products Laboratory show that when decay or other abnormal environmental factors are not present, wood does not deteriorate in strength or stiffness from age alone for periods of 100 years or more. Limited tests conducted on a few timbers from Japanese temples 3 to 13 centuries old indicate that shock resistance is seriously reduced after several centuries, but effects on the other structural properties are small.

In spite of the permanence of the wood-frame house, many older houses are being razed, or abandoned and left to a slower destruction by decay, insects, rodents, and the elements. Some of these houses have deteriorated to a point where rehabilitation would be impractical; but many could be restored to a sound condition and updated in convenience and comfort at a lower cost than that required to build a new house (fig. 1). In addition to monetary savings, rehabilitation has other advantages: The owner can stay in familiar surroundings; some older houses provide more space than can be achieved in a new house at reasonable cost; the work can usually be done as finances become available; and the character of the older house is often preferred to that of a new one. Finally, one of the most important aspects of rehabilitation is conservation of our timber resource.

For many years the Department of Agriculture, specifically through the Forest Service, has been concerned with wise use of the Nation's timber resource. And because so large a part of the timber harvest goes into housing, it is understandable that research on phases of wood house construction has long been a part of the Forest Products Laboratory program.

This Appraisal portion of the handbook presents information based on this research as a guide to appraising the suitability of a house for rehabilitation. It relates only to the condition of the house itself, not to an area. Once a house is deemed suitable for rehabilitation, suggestions on how to proceed are covered in the Rehabilitation portion.

Whether or not a house is worth rehabilitating can be substantiated only by systematically inspecting the house and evaluating any necessary repairs in comparison with the value of the finished product. If the foundation is good and the floor, wall, and roof framing are structurally sound, the house probably is worth rehabilitating; but a thorough inspection is still in order.

Examination of the house is treated here by elements to provide a systematic approach to evaluation. Although no publication could possibly cover every condition that might exist in houses of varying age, style, and geographic location, several general considerations should cover most situations in a wood-frame house. General suggestions are also given for examining heating, plumbing, and electrical systems; but in these areas professional help will probably be desirable. Some contractors will assist in determining the condition of the house and repairs or replacements required. Also, code requirements vary and what seemed to be a minor addition or repair may become a major revamping of the entire structure for code compliance. In most communities a building official will inspect the house and indicate code violations.

MASONRY AND CONCRETE

FOUNDATIONS

The most important component of a house from a rehabilitation standpoint is the foundation. It supports the entire house, and failure can have far-reaching effects. Check the foundation for general deterioration that may allow moisture or water to enter the basement and may require expensive repairs. More importantly, check for uneven settlement (fig. 2). Uneven settlement will distort the house frame or even pull it apart. This distortion may rack window and door frames out of square, loosen interior finish and siding, and create cracks that permit infiltration of cold air. A single localized failure or minor settling can be corrected by releveling of beams or floor joists and is not a sufficient reason to reject the house. Numerous failures and general uneven settlement, however, would indicate a

1

Figure 1.—Many types and sizes of houses may be suitable for some degree of rehabilitation. Owners may see a variety of ways to put into practice the principles listed in this publication.

new foundation is required or, more critically, that the house is probably unsuitable for rehabilitation.

MASONRY WALLS AND PIERS

Many old houses have stone or brick foundations, and some may be supported on masonry piers. Check the masonry foundation for cracks and crumbling mortar, a common defect that can usually be repaired, depending on its extent. More extensive deterioration may indicate the need for major repair or replacement.

Crawl space houses usually have a foundation wall or piers supporting the floor joists. These supports must be checked for cracks and settlement the same as the perimeter foundation.

WOOD PIERS

Occasionally houses will be on pier-type wood post foundations. These are more common in certain areas of the country. Such foundations give good service if the wood is properly preservatively treated. However, in the inspection they must be checked for decay and insect damage.

CONCRETE WALLS

Most foundation walls of poured concrete have minor hairline cracks that have little effect on the structure; however, open cracks indicate a failure that may get progressively worse. Whether a crack is active or dormant can be determined only by observation over several months.

DAMP BASEMENTS

Damp or leaky basement walls may require a major repair, especially if the basement space is to be used. Possible causes of the dampness are clogged drain tile, clogged or broken downspouts, cracks in walls, lack of slope of the finished grade away from the house foundation, or a high water table. Check for dampness by examining the basement a few hours after a heavy rain.

The most common source of dampness is surface water, such as from downspouts discharging directly at the foundation wall or from surface drainage flowing directly against the foundation wall. Therefore the cardinal rule is to keep water away from the foundation, and this is best accomplished by proper grading.

A high water table is a more serious problem. There is little possibility of achieving a dry basement if the water table is high or periodically high. Heavy foundation waterproofing or footing drains may help but, since the source cannot be controlled, it is unlikely they will do more than minimize the problem.

MASONRY VENEERS

Uneven settlement of the foundation will cause cracks in brick or stone veneer. Cracks can be grouted and joints

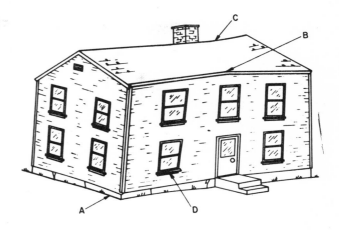

M-142 839

Figure 2.—Uneven foundation settlement, A, may result in a house badly out of square. Evidences may include B, eaveline distortion; C, sagging roof ridge; or D, loosefitting frames or even binding windows or doors.

repointed, but large or numerous cracks will be unsightly even after they are patched. The mortar also may be weak and crumbling, and joints may be incompletely filled or poorly finished. If these faults are limited to a small area, regrouting or repointing is feasible. For improved appearance, the veneer can be sandblasted.

It is important to prevent water from entering the masonry wall or flowing over the face of the wall in any quantity. Examine flashing or calking at all projecting trim, copings, sills, and intersections of roof and walls. Plan to repair any of these places where flashing or calking is not provided or where need of repair is apparent.

Porous or soft brick or stone should be coated with a clear water repellent after care has been taken to see that no water can get behind the veneer.

CHIMNEYS AND FIREPLACES

The most obvious defect to look for in a chimney is cracks in the masonry or loose mortar. Such cracks are usually the result of foundation settlement or the attachment of television antennas or other items that put undue stress on the chimney. These cracks are a particular hazard if the flue does not have a fireproof lining.

The chimney should be supported on its own footing. It should not be supported by the framework of the house. Look in the attic to see that ceiling and roof framing are no closer than 2 inches to the chimney. Either of these defects are fire hazards and should be corrected immediately.

If the house has a fireplace, check to see if it has an operating damper. Where no damper exists, one should be added to prevent heat loss up the flue when the fireplace is not in use. A fireplace that looks like it has been used a lot probably draws well; however, you can check this by lighting a few sheets of newspaper on the hearth. A good fireplace will draw immediately; a usable one will draw after about a minute.

3

STRUCTURAL WOOD FRAME

The building frame should be carefully examined to see if it is distorted from foundation failure or from improper or inadequate framing. It should also be checked for decay and insect damage. (These last two items are treated on page 7.)

FLOOR SUPPORTS

In a basement house, interior support is usually provided by wood or steel girders supported on wood or steel posts. Wood posts should be supported on pedestals and not be embedded in the concrete floor, where they may take on moisture and decay. Examine the base of the wood posts for decay even if they are set above the floor slab. Steel posts are normally supported on metal plates. Check the wood girders for sag and also for decay at the exterior wall bearings. Sag is permanent deflection that can be noted especially near the middle of a structural member (fig. 3). Some sag is common in permanently loaded wood beams and is not a problem unless parts of the house have obviously distorted. Sag is usually an appearance problem rather than a structural problem. Some deflection is normal and about 3/8-inch deflection in a 10-foot span girder is acceptable in design.

FLOOR FRAMING

The sill plates, or joists and headers where sill plates are not used, rest on top of the foundation. Thus they are

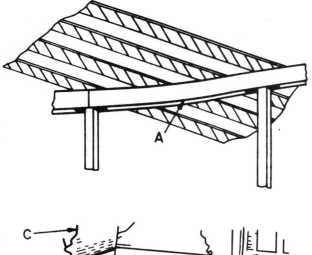

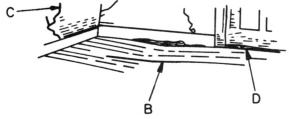

M-142 840

Figure 3.—Sagging horizontal member, A, has resulted in: B, uneven floor; C, cracked plaster; and D, poorly fitting door.

exposed to moisture and are vulnerable to decay or insect attack. Examine these members specifically, as well as the entire floor framing system for decay and insect damage, particularly if the basement or crawl space is very damp.

Joists, like girders, should be examined for sag. Here too some sag can be expected and is not a sign of structural damage. It is usually not a serious problem in floor joists unless the foundation system has settled unevenly, causing excessive deflection in parts of the floor system. Look for local deflection due to inadequate support of a heavy partition load that runs parallel to the joists. Sag might be considered excessive if it is readily apparent from a visual appraisal of the levelness of a floor.

A floor may be noted to be excessively springy when walking across it. This may be remedied by adding extra joists or girders to increase stiffness.

Another point of particular concern is the framing of the floor joists around stair openings. Some builders estimate that 50 percent of the houses built have inadequate framing around stairs. Check floors around the opening for levelness. Where floors are sagging, the framing will have to be carefully leveled and reinforced.

WALL FRAMING

The usual stud wall normally has much more than adequate strength. It may be distorted, however, for reasons covered in preceding sections. Check openings for squareness by operating doors and windows and observing fit. Some adjustments are possible but large distortions will require new framing. Also check for sag in headers over wide window openings or wide openings between rooms. Where the sag is visually noticeable, new headers will be required.

ROOF FRAMING

Examine the roof for sagging of the ridge, the rafters, and the sheathing. This is easily done by visual observation. If the ridge line is not straight or the roof does not appear to be in a uniform plane, some repair may be necessary. The ridge will sag due to improper support, inadequate ties at the plate level, or even from sagging of the rafters. Rafters will sag due to inadequate stiffness or because they were not well seasoned. Sheathing sag may indicate too wide a spacing between rafters or strip sheathing, or plywood that is too thin or has delaminated.

EXTERIOR

Exterior wood on a house will last many years if it is kept free of moisture and is given reasonable care.

SIDING AND TRIM

The main problems with siding and trim stem from excessive moisture, which can enter from either inside or

Figure 4.—Signs of excessive water damage are evident in the paint peeling of this window sill and sash and broken calking around the window.

outside. One of the main contributors to the problem is the lack of roof overhang, allowing rain to run down the face of the wall. Moisture may also enter from the inside, because of the lack of a vapor barrier, and subsequently condense within the wall.

Look for space between horizontal siding boards by standing very close and sighting along the wall. Some cracks can be calked, but a general gapping or looseness may indicate new siding is required. If the boards are not badly warped, renailing may solve the problem. Check siding for decay where two boards are butted end to end, at corners, and around window and door frames.

Decorative trim is sometimes excessive and presents unusual decay and maintenance problems, particularly where water may be trapped.

Good shingle siding appears as a perfect mosaic, whereas worn shingles have an allover ragged appearance and close examination will show individual shingles to be broken, warped, and upturned. New siding will be required if shingles are badly weathered or worn.

WINDOWS

Windows usually present one of the more difficult problems of old wood-frame houses (fig. 4). If they are loose fitting and not weatherstripped, they will be a major source of uncomfortable drafts and cause high heat loss. Check the tightness of fit and examine the sash and the sill for decay. Also check the operation of the window. Casement windows should be checked for warp at top and bottom.

When replacement of windows is planned, check the window dimensions. If the window is not a standard size or if a different size is desired, the opening will have to be reframed or new sash must be made, both of which are expensive.

In cold climates windows should be double glazed or have storm windows, both to reduce heat loss and avoid condensation. Again, if the windows are not a standard size, storm windows may be expensive.

DOORS

Exterior doors should fit well without sticking. They should be weather-stripped to avoid air infiltration, but this is a very simple item to add. Difficulties in latching a door can usually be attributed to warping. A simple adjustment of the latch keeper will solve the problem in some instances, but badly warped doors should be replaced.

Storm doors are necessary in cold climates not only for heat saving and comfort, but also to avoid moisture condensation on or in the door and to protect the door from severe weather.

If the door frame is out of square due to foundation settlement or other racking of the house frame, the opening will probably have to be reframed.

The lower parts of exterior doors and storm doors are particularly susceptible to decay and should be carefully checked. Also observe the condition of the threshold, which may be worn, weathered, or decayed, and require replacement.

PORCHES

One of the components of a house most vulnerable to decay and insect attack is the porch. Since it is open to the weather, windblown rain or snow can easily raise the moisture content of wood members to conditions for promoting growth of wood-destroying organisms. Steps are often placed in contact with soil, always a poor practice with untreated wood.

Check all wood members for decay and insect damage. Give particular attention to the base of posts or any place where two members join and water might get into the joint. Decay often occurs where posts are not raised above the porch floor to allow air to dry out the base of the post. It may be worthwhile to replace a few members, but the porch that is in a generally deteriorated condition should be completely rebuilt or removed.

FINISHES

Failure of exterior finishes on siding or trim results most commonly from excessive moisture in the wood. This may

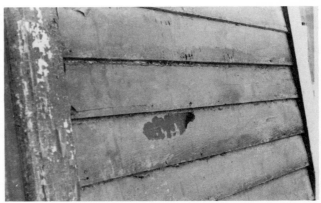

Figure 5.—Excessive paint peeling on siding.

result either from direct rain or from moisture vapor condensing in the walls. Finish failures may also be caused by poor paints, improper application of good paints, poor surface preparation, or incompatible successive coatings.

Excessive peeling (fig. 5) may require complete removal of the paint. Since this can be very expensive, re-siding may be considered.

ROOF

If the roof is actually leaking, it should be obvious from damage inside the house. A look in the attic may also reveal water stains on the rafters, indicating small leaks that will eventually cause damage. Damage inside the house is not always attributable to roofing, but could be caused by faulty flashing or result from condensation.

ASPHALT SHINGLES

Asphalt shingles are the most common roof covering and are made in a wide range of weights and thicknesses. The most obvious deterioration of asphalt shingles is loss of the surface granules. The shingles may also become quite brittle. More important, however, is the wear that occurs in the narrow grooves between the tabs or sections of the shingle, or between two consecutive shingles in a row. This wear may extend completely through to the roof boards without being apparent from a casual visual inspection. A good asphalt shingle should last 18 to 20 years.

WOOD SHINGLES

Wood shingles also find considerable use for covering of pitched roofs and are most commonly of durable woods such as cedar in No. 1 or No. 2 grades. A good wood shingle roof should appear as a perfect mosaic, whereas a roof with worn shingles has an allover ragged appearance. Individual shingles on the worn roof are broken, warped, and upturned. The roof with this worn appearance should be completely replaced even though there is no evidence of leaking. Excessive shade may cause fungus growth and early shingle deterioration. A good wood shingle roof will last up to 30 years under favorable conditions.

BUILT-UP ROOFING

Built-up roofing on flat- or low-sloped roofs should be examined by going onto the roof and looking for bare spots in the surfacing and for separations and breaks in the felt. Bubbles, blisters, or soft spots also indicate that the roof needs major repairs. Alligatoring patterns on smooth-surface built-up roofs may not be a failure of the roof. The life of a built-up roof varies from 15 to 30 years, depending on number of layers of felt and quality of application.

FLASHING

Flashing should be evident where the roof intersects walls, chimneys, or vents, and where two roofs intersect to form a valley. Check for corroded flashing that should be replaced to prevent future problems. Likewise, check for corroded gutters and downspouts, which can be restored by repainting unless severely corroded.

OVERHANG

If the house was built with no roof overhang, the addition of an overhang should be considered in the remodeling plan. It will greatly reduce maintenance on siding and window trim, and prolong the life of both.

INTERIOR

Interior surfaces deteriorate due to wear, distortion of the structure, and the presence of moisture. Sometimes the problem is further complicated by the use of cheap or improper materials, improper application of wall coatings or floor surfaces, or excessive layers of wallpaper.

FLOORING

WOOD FLOORS

In checking wood floors look for buckling or cupping of boards that can result from high moisture content of the boards or wetting of the floor. Also notice if the boards are separated due to shrinkage. This shrinkage is more probable if the flooring boards are wide. If the floor is generally smooth and without excessive separation between boards, refinishing may put it in good condition; however, be sure there is enough thickness left in the flooring to permit sanding. Most flooring cannot be sanded more than two or three times; if it is softwood flooring without a subfloor, even one sanding might weaken the floor too much. Sanding of plywood block floors should also be quite limited. If floors have wide cracks or are too thin to sand, some type of new flooring will have to be added.

RESILIENT TILE

Floors with resilient tile should be examined for loose tile, cracks between tile, broken corners, and chipped edges. Look to see if any ridges or unevenness in the underlayment are showing through. Replacement of any tile in a room may necessitate replacing the flooring in the whole room because tile change color with age and new tile will not match the old.

WALLS AND CEILINGS

INTERIOR COVERING

The interior wall covering in old houses is usually plaster, but may be gypsum board in more recently built homes. Wood paneling may also be found but is usually limited to one room or to a single wall or accent area.

Plaster almost always has some hairlines cracks, even when it is in good condition. Minor cracks and holes can be patched, but a new wall covering should be applied if large cracks and holes are numerous, if the surface is generally uneven and bulging, or if the plaster is loose in spots. The same general rule applies to ceilings.

If walls have been papered, check the thickness of the paper. If more than two or three layers of paper are present, they should be removed before applying new paper, and all wallpaper should be removed before painting.

PAINTED SURFACES

The paint on painted surfaces may have been built up to excessive thickness. It may be chipped due to mechanical damage, to incompatibility between successive layers, or to improper surface preparation prior to repainting. Old kalsomine surfaces may require considerable labor to recondition, so a new wall covering should be considered. Paint failures may be due to application of paint over kalsomine.

TRIM, CABINETS, AND DOORS

Trim should have tight joints and fit closely to walls. If the finish is worn but the surface is smooth, refinishing may be feasible. If the finish is badly chipped or checked, removing it will be laborious regardless of whether the new finish is to be a clear sealer or paint. Trim or cabinetry of plain design will be less difficult to prepare for refinishing than that having ornately carved designs.

If any trim is damaged or it is necessary to move doors or windows, all trim in the room may have to be replaced as it may be difficult to match the existing trim. Small sections

of special trim might be custom made but the cost should be compared with complete replacement. Check with the building supply dealer to see if the particular trim is still being made. Also check some of the older cabinet shops to see if they have shaper knives of this trim design.

The problems with interior doors are much the same as those for exterior doors except there are no decay or threshold problems.

RECOGNIZING DAMAGE BY DECAY AND INSECTS

DECAY

Look for decay in any part of the house that is subject to prolonged wetting. Decay thrives in a mild temperature and in wood with a high moisture content.

One indication of decay in wood is abnormal color and loss of sheen. The brown color may be deeper than normal (fig. 6A), and in advanced stages cubical checking and collapse occur (fig. 6B). The abnormal color may also be a lightening which eventually progresses to a bleached appearance (fig. 7). Fine black lines may be present with the bleached appearance.

Fungal growths appearing as strandlike or cottony masses on the surface of wood indicate excessive water and consequently the presence of decay (fig. 8).

The visual methods of detecting decay do not show the extent of damage. The two strength properties severely reduced by decay are hardness and toughness. Prod the wood with a sharp tool and observe resistance to marring. To determine loss of hardness compare this resistance with that of sound wood. Sound wood tends to lift out as one or two relatively long slivers, and breaks are splintery. To determine loss of toughness use a pointed tool to jab the

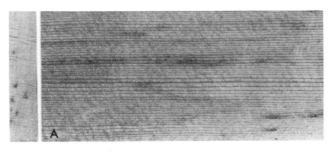

M-124 928

Figure 6.—A, Discolored wood showing advanced stages of decay; B, cubical checking and collapse.

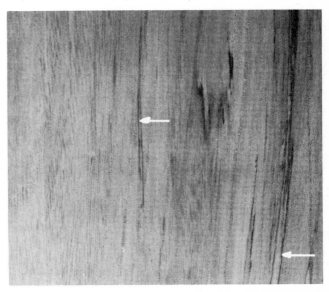

M-124 927

Figure 7.—Lightening of wood with fine black lines showing decay.

Figure 8.—Fungal surface growth in crawl space area under joist. (Pen shows comparative size.)

wood and pry out a sliver. If toughness has been greatly reduced by decay, the wood breaks squarely across the grain with little splintering and lifts out with little resistance.

Decay may exist in any part of the house, but some areas are particularly vulnerable. Special attention should be given to these areas:

FOUNDATIONS AND FLOORS

Decay often starts in framing members near the foundation. It may be detected by papery, fanlike growths that are initially white with a yellow tinge, and turn brown or black with age. Look for these growths between subfloor and finish floor and between joists and subfloor. They may become exposed by shrinkage of flooring during dry weather. These growths may also exist under carpets, in cupboards, or in other protected areas that tend to stay damp.

SIDING AND EXTERIOR TRIM

Where siding is close to the ground, look for discoloration, checking, or softening. Also check for signs of decay where siding ends butt against each other or against trim.

ROOF SYSTEM

Observe wood shingles for cubical checking, softening, and breakage of the exposed ends. Asphalt shingles have deteriorated if they can be easily pulled apart between the fingers. Edges of roofs are particularly vulnerable if not properly flashed. If the roofing is deteriorating, check the underside of the roof sheathing for evidence of condensation or decay.

PORCHES

Give particular attention to step treads or deck surfaces that are checked or concavely worn so they trap water. Also check joints in railings or posts. Enclosed porches may have condensation occurring on the underside of the deck and framing. Check the crawl space for signs of dampness and examine areas where these signs occur.

WINDOWS AND DOORS

Look for brown or black discoloration near joints or failure of nearby paint (fig. 9). Both are signs of possible decay. Also check the inside for water stains on the sash and

Figure 9.—Stain and decay may occur at such joints in a window frame.

Figure 10.—Termite shelter tubes on foundation.

sill resulting from condensation running down the glass. Where these stains exist, check for softening and molding.

INSECT PROBLEMS

The three major kinds of wood-attacking insects that cause problems in wood-frame houses are termites, powder-post beetles, and carpenter ants. Methods of recognizing each of these are discussed under separate headings. Where there is any indication of one of these insects, probe the wood with a sharp tool to determine the extent of damage.

TERMITES

There are two main classifications of termites: (1) Subterranean termites, which have access to the ground or other water source, and (2) nonsubterranean termites, which do not require direct access to water.

Examine all areas close to the ground for subterranean termites. One of the most obvious signs is earthen tubes (fig. 10) built over the surface of foundation walls to provide runways from the soil to the wood above. Termites may also enter through cracks or voids in the foundations or concrete floors. They do not require runways to the soil where there is a source of water such as a plumbing leak.

Another sign of the presence of termites is the swarming of winged adults early in the spring or fall. Termites resemble ants, but the termites have much longer wings and do not have the thin waist of an ant (fig. 11). Where there is an indication of termites, look for galleries that follow the grain of the wood, usually leaving a shell of sound wood (fig. 12).

Nonsubterranean termites live in damp or dry wood without outside moisture or contact with the ground. Look for these only in Hawaii and in a narrow coastal strip extending from central California to Virginia. One of the early signs of these termites is sandlike excretory pellets that are discarded outside the wood. Nonsubterranean termites can also be identified by the presence of swarming winged forms. They cut freely across the grain of the wood rather than following the grain as the subterranean termites do.

To combat termites, soil poisoning is often recommended, but this is generally done by a professional exterminator.

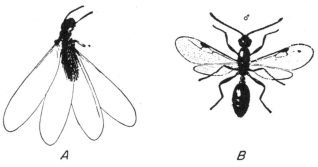

M–137 348

Figure 11.—Differences between winged termite, A; and winged ant, B.

POWDER-POST BEETLES

Powder-post beetles are most easily recognized by their borings, which are about the consistency of flour. Many borings remain inside the wood. The adults leave the wood through a hole about the diameter of a pencil lead, giving the wood the appearance of having been hit by birdshot. Such holes may be just the result of a previous infestation, so check for fresh, clean sawdust as a sign of current activity. Activity may also be recognized by the rasping sound the beetles make while tunneling.

Look for powder-post beetles in humid locations such as near the ground. Sometimes the homeowner may destroy them with an approved insecticide, but in severe cases, fumigation by a professional exterminator is required.

CARPENTER ANTS

The presence of carpenter ants is often discovered by their chewed wood, which resembles coarse sawdust and is placed in piles outside the wood. They do not eat the wood, but only nest in it. Working ants may be as much as half an inch long. They make a rustling noise in walls, floors, or woodwork. Look for signs of carpenter ants in softwood in high humidity locations.

An approved insecticide blown into the galleries will destroy carpenter ants. Eliminating the high moisture situation will prevent a recurrence.

INSULATION AND CONTROL OF MOISTURE

Good insulation cuts heating costs and adds to comfort by making the temperature in the house more uniform. Humidification increases comfort and saves fuel by reducing the temperature level required for comfort. While both

F–494 578

Figure 12.—Termite damage to interior of a pine 2 by 4.

9

insulation and humidification are desirable, their addition to older homes without vapor barriers in walls and ceilings may create moisture condensation problems. Where large differences exist between indoor and outdoor temperatures, pressure forces water vapor out through the walls.

In the uninsulated house this vapor usually moves on to the outside without any problem. Where insulation is added, the dewpoint often occurs within the insulation, so water vapor condenses into free water with consequent wet insulation and siding. In some instances where indoor relative humidities are low and the outside covering material allows moisture in the walls to escape readily, no moisture problems may result. However, mechanical humidification, in addition to normal moisture from cooking, bathing, and respiration, amplifies moisture problems; the water vapor pressure drive is increased and consequently the rate of moisture movement into the walls. Vapor barriers in walls and ceilings reduce the rate of moisture movement into these areas and thus help to control the moisture problems otherwise created by adding insulation or humidification.

INSULATION

Look in the attic to determine the amount of ceiling insulation present. The ceiling represents the greatest source of heat loss on cool days as well as the greatest source of heat gain on warm days. At least 3 inches of insulation should be provided for homes in mild climates and 4 to 6 inches for those in cold climates. To find out if the walls are insulated, some siding and sheathing or interior covering must be removed. Insulation in walls should be included in any house rehabilitation in cold climates and in warm climates where summer cooling is essential. Insulation is also needed under floors of crawl space houses in cold climates.

VAPOR BARRIERS

Vapor barriers should be provided on the warm side of all insulation. Most houses built before the mid–1930's do not have vapor barriers. If the ceiling insulation is in blanket form with a covering around it, the covering material may resist the passage of moisture. However, if the ceiling is loose fill, look under it for a separate vapor barrier of coated or laminated paper, aluminum foil, or plastic film. The same thing is true of insulated walls, where the vapor barrier should be on the inside of the walls.

Check in crawl spaces for a vapor barrier laid on top of the soil. If there is none and the crawl space seems quite damp, a vapor barrier could be added.

There is no convenient way to determine if there are vapor barriers under floor slabs. If the floor seems damp most of the time, there probably is no vapor barrier. A barrier would then have to be added on top of the slab, with a new finish floor applied over it, to have a dry finish floor.

VENTILATION

The two major areas where good ventilation is required are the attic, or roof joist spaces in the case of a cathedral ceiling or flatroofed house, and the crawl space. The general adequacy of existing ventilation can be observed just from the degree of dampness.

Moisture passes into the attic from the house and condenses as the air cools down or where the moist air contacts the cold roof members. Both inlet and outlet vents must be located properly for good circulation of air through all the attic area. These vents not only help keep the attic dry in winter, but keep hot air moving from the attic during summer and help to cool the house.

Observe the size and location of crawl space vents. There should be at least four vents located near building corners for optimum cross ventilation and minimum dead air space.

MECHANICAL

Because many of the plumbing, heating, and wiring systems in a house are concealed, it may be difficult to determine their adequacy. For the same reason it is difficult to make major changes without considerable cutting of wall surfaces and, in some situations, even structural members.

In a very old house the mechanical systems may have to be replaced and this will become a major cost item. At the same time, however, properly installed new systems will be responsible to a large extent for comfort and convenience in the house. One bonus can be the dramatic recovery of space and improvement in the appearance of the basement when an old "octopus" gravity warm air heating system is replaced by a modern forced-air system.

Code provisions relating to mechanical systems should be carefully checked.

PLUMBING

WATER SUPPLY SYSTEM

Water pressure is important. Check several faucets to see if the flow is adequate. Low pressure can result from various causes. The service may be too small or it may be reduced in diameter due to lime, particularly with very old lead service pipes. A $3/4$-inch inside diameter service is considered adequate.

The main distribution pipes should be $3/4$-inch inside diameter but branch lines may be $1/2$-inch inside diameter. Sizes can be checked easily. Copper pipes $1/2$-inch inside diameter are $5/8$-inch outside diameter, and $3/4$-inch inside diameter pipes are $7/8$-inch outside diameter. Galvanized pipes $1/2$-inch inside diameter are $7/8$-inch outside diameter and pipes $3/4$-inch inside diameter are $1^1/8$-inch outside diameter.

The supply pressure may be inadequate. If the house has its own water system, check the gage on the pressure tank, which should read a minimum of 20 and preferably 40 to 50 pounds. Anything less will indicate the pump is not operating properly, or the pressure setting is too low. If the supply is from a municipal system, the pressure in the mains may be too low, though this is unlikely.

Check shutoff valves at the service entrance and at various points in the system to determine if they have become frozen with age or little use.

Check for leaks in the water supply system. Rust or white or greenish crusting of pipe or joints may indicate leaks.

Water hammer may be a problem. This results from stopping the water flowing in the pipe by abruptly closing a faucet. Air chambers placed on the supply lines at the fixtures usually absorb the shock and prevent water hammer. If there is water hammer, air chambers may be waterlogged. If there are no air chambers, they may be added.

The water from any private well should be tested even though the well has been in continuous use.

PLUMBING DRAINAGE SYSTEM

The drainage system consists of the sewer lateral, the underfloor drains, the drainage pipes above the floor, and the vents. Pipes may have become clogged or broken or they may be of inadequate size. Venting in particular may be inadequate and far below code requirements.

Flush fixtures to see if drains are sluggish. If so, check the following:

Old laterals are commonly of vitreous bell tile. These may have been poorly installed or become broken, allowing tree roots to enter at the breaks or through the joints. Roots can be removed mechanically but this operation may have to be repeated every few years.

The underfloor drains may be of tile or even of steel and could be broken or rusted out. They may have become clogged and only need cleaning.

The drainage system above the basement floor or within the house should be checked for adequacy and leaks.

Vents may be inadequate or may have become clogged; in extreme cases they may cause the water in the traps to be siphoned out, allowing sewer gas to enter the house. Note any excessive suction when a toilet is flushed.

REQUIRED ADDITIONS

Additional supply and drain lines may be desirable in modernizing a house. New lines may be required for automatic washers, added baths, adequate sill cocks, or in reorganizing the layout.

WATER HEATER

With a hot water heating system, water may also be heated satisfactorily for cooking, bathing, and other personal needs. However, in a hot air furnace, the water heating coil seldom provides enough hot water. Furthermore, during summer months when the hot air heating is not needed, a separate system is required to provide hot water. A gas water heater should have at least a 30—gallon capacity and preferably more. An electric water heater should have a capacity of 50 gallons or more.

FIXTURES

Plumbing fixtures that are quite old may be rust stained and require replacement, or it may be desirable to replace them just for appearance.

SEWAGE DISPOSAL

Drainage may not be adequate. Run water for a few minutes to check for clogged drain lines between the house and the sewer main. If a private sewage system exists, consider the adequacy of the drain field. If a new drainage field is needed, some codes require percolation tests of soil.

HEATING

Heating system advances and concepts of comfort outdate the heating systems in most old houses. Central heating with heat piped to all rooms is considered a necessity in all but very small houses.

The only way to satisfactorily check the adequacy of the heating system is through use. If the system is adequate for the desired degree of comfort, check the furnace or boiler for overall general condition.

GRAVITY WARM AIR

Gravity warm air systems are common in older homes. Some gravity warm air furnaces may heat a house relatively well, but it is doubtful that the temperature control and heat distribution will be as good as with a forced-circulation system.

If a warm air system is exceptionally dirty, there may be bad smudges above the registers. This will indicate some repair work is required; if the furnace is old, it may need to be replaced. Rusty ducts may need replacement.

FLOOR FURNACE

Warm air floor furnaces may be adequate for small houses.

GRAVITY STEAM

One-pipe gravity steam heating systems are common in older homes. The system is similar in appearance to hot water. This is an extremely simple system and, if properly installed, it will provide adequate heat but with no great speed or control. It can be modernized without basic changes merely by replacing standing radiators with baseboard heaters.

A one-pipe gravity steam system can be made more positive in action by converting to a two-pipe system. This requires adding traps and return lines.

A two-pipe steam system can be modified to a circulating hot water system. Circulating pumps must be added but this results in greater speed of heat distribution and excellent control.

RADIANT

Radiant heat from hot water flowing through coils embedded in concrete floors or plastered ceilings is less common but may provide excellent heating. Such systems may become airlocked and require an expert to restore proper operation. Breaks in ceiling coils can be repaired fairly easily but repairing breaks in floors is extremely difficult. If floor breaks are extensive, the system will probably need to be replaced.

ELECTRIC PANEL

The electric heating panels have no moving parts to wear out and should be in good condition unless a heating element has burned out.

ELECTRICAL

The service is the first thing to check. So many new electrical appliances have come into common use in recent years that old houses may not have adequate wiring to accommodate them, particularly if air conditioning is installed. The service should be at least 100 amperes for the average three-bedroom house. If the house is large or if air conditioning is added, the service should be 200 amps. If the main distribution panel has room for circuits, additional circuits can be added to supply power where there is a shortage. Otherwise another distribution panel may be added.

Examine electrical wiring wherever possible. Some wiring is usually exposed in the attic or basement. Wiring should also be checked at several wall receptacles or fixtures. If any armored cable or conduit is badly rusted, or if wiring or cable insulation is deteriorated, damaged, brittle or crumbly, the house wiring has probably deteriorated from age or overloading and should be replaced.

At least one electrical outlet on each wall of a room and two or more on long walls is desirable but may not always be necessary. Ceiling lights should have a wall switch, and rooms without a ceiling light should have a wall switch for at least one outlet.

GENERAL CONSIDERATIONS [1]

The value of the house being considered for reconditioning, and the convenience and pleasure of using it over many years will be affected by the layout and appearance. Some points to consider are relationship and convenience of areas to each other, traffic circulation, privacy, and adequacy of room size. Conceivably some houses will not lend themselves to an ideal arrangement without excessive cost, and adequate living conditions may be possible with some sacrifice in arrangement.

CIRCULATION

Observe circulation or traffic patterns. For good circulation the general rule is to keep through-traffic from all rooms or at least keep traffic at one side of a room rather than through its center. If circulation is a problem, it can sometimes be improved simply by moving doors to the corners of rooms or by placing furniture in a manner to direct traffic where it will be least objectionable. Traffic

considerations will be discussed further as they relate to specific areas.

LAYOUT

Ideally, houses should have rooms arranged in three areas—the private or bedroom area, the work area consisting of kitchen and utility rooms, and the relaxation area consisting of dining and living rooms. A family room, a den, or a recreation room may exist in or between these general areas. The den should be out of the general circulation areas and, if it is part of the bedroom area, may double as a guest room. A recreation room in the basement can serve some of the same functions as a family room. The relationship of areas will be treated further as each area is discussed.

WORK AREA

The location of the kitchen in relation to other areas of the house is one of the most critical. It should have direct access to the dining area and be accessible to the garage or driveway for ease in unloading groceries. Being near the utility room is also convenient as the housewife often has work in progress in the kitchen and utility room at the same time. Traffic should not pass through the kitchen work area, i.e., the range-refrigerator-sink triangle.

The size of the kitchen is important. There was a period when kitchens were made very small with the idea that this was convenient, but the many modern appliances that now commonly go into a kitchen, as well as the inclusion of a breakfast area, require much more space. If the kitchen is too small, a major addition or alteration will be necessary.

A coat closet near the kitchen entrance and some facility for washing up near the work area are desirable. However, in the small house neither may be feasible.

PRIVATE AREA

The bedroom and bathroom area should be separated as much as possible, both visually and acoustically from the living and work areas.

Every bedroom should be accessible to a bathroom without going through another room, and at least one bathroom should be accessible to work and relaxation areas without going through a bedroom. One of the basic rules of privacy is to avoid traffic through one bedroom to another. If this privacy is not presently provided, some changes in layout may be desirable.

Check the size of bedrooms. It is desirable to have a floor area of at least 125 square feet for a double bed and 150 square feet for twin beds. Smaller bedrooms can be very usable, but consider limitations for furnishing them.

---

[1] This section could not possibly cover all items to be considered in evaluting a home for rehabilitation. Thus the attention here is focused on the building itself, with no mention of problems that relate to a particular site. It is beyond the scope of this handbook to get into such problems—important as they might be—as the condition and future of the neighborhood, availability of transportation, distance to shopping and schools, or the vulnerability to such natural disasters as floods.

RELAXATION AREA

The relaxation area is usually at the front of an older house, but rooms at the side or rear may be used, particularly if this provides a view into a landscaped yard. If the house has a small parlor or a living room and dining room separated by an arch, consider removing partitions or arches to give a more spacious feeling. The main entrance is usually at or near the living area. Check for a coat closet near this entrance, and a passage into the work area without passing through the living room or at least not more than a corner or end of the room.

APPEARANCE

Taste is largely a personal matter so only basic guidelines will be given. Simplicity and unity are the major considerations. A good "period" style may be worth preserving and a house possessing the quality commonly referred to as "charm" may be appraised $2,000 to $3,000 higher than plainer ones. Style or charm can assume less importance, however, after you live for awhile with inconvenience, discomforts, and constant repairs.

Simplicity is one of the first principles. Observe the main lines of the house. Some variety adds interest, but numerous roof lines at a variety of slopes present a busy, confused appearance. Strong horizontal lines are usually desirable in a conventional residence to give the appearance of being "tied to the ground." Strong vertical lines tend to make a house look tall and unstable.

List the number of materials used as siding. There should never be more than three, and not more than two would be preferable. Look at the trim and see if it seems to belong with the house or is just stuck on as ornamentation.

Unity is as important as simplicity. The house should appear as a unit, not as a cluster of unrelated components. Windows and trim should be in keeping with the style of the house. Windows should be of the same type and of a very limited number of sizes. Shutters should be one-half the width of the window so that, if closed, they would cover the window. Porches and garages should blend with the house rather than appear as attachments.

If the dwellings appears unattractive, consider how paint and landscaping may affect it. Even an attractive house will not look good without being properly painted or landscaped.

FINAL EVALUATION

After the house has been completely examined and all repair requirements listed, the information should be carefully evaluated. Some general guides for evaluating the information are presented here; however, judgment will be required to draw conclusions from these guides.

MAJOR REASONS FOR REJECTION

Throughout the discussion some major reasons for rejection have been given. These are restated here:

1. The foundation may be completely unrepairable. Houses are occasionally moved onto a new foundation, but this is generally not economical unless the house is otherwise in extremely good condition.

2. If the entire frame of the house is badly out of square, or if the framing is generally decayed or termite infested, the house is probably not worth rehabilitating.

3. If there are numerous replacements, or major repairs and replacements combined, the suitability for rehabilitation is questionable.

GUIDEPOSTS FOR THE FINAL DECISION

If the foundation and frame are in reasonable condition, and the repair and replacement items do not appear excessive, base a final decision on the following factors:

COST

If the cost of buying and rehabilitating the house does not exceed the fair market value of houses in the area, it is a sound investment. A general rule-of-thumb for a house presently owned is that the rehabilitation cost should not exceed two-thirds of the cost of a comparable new house. The cost can be arrived at in two ways:

A. If the work is to be done on a fixed price contract, the contractor's bid will give you a definite figure. However, this figure should be increased about 10 percent for unforeseen extras.

B. If you plan to do most of the work and are concerned with the economics of the project, first get bids on those items that will be done by others. Second, figure the cost of all materials for work you would do. Third, estimate your labor time and establish costs using a fair hourly rate. If you are not experienced in building construction, increase your labor estimate by 50 percent because much time is lost in doing work a little at a time, and also there is a strong tendency to underestimate.

LOCATION

A particularly good location would be justification for spending more; a generally undesirable or deteriorating location would indicate much less than two-thirds the new house cost should be spent.

SENTIMENTAL VALUE

If there are sentimental attachments, the value of the rehabilitated house must be decided by the individual concerned. However, neither the finance company nor a prospective buyer will allow anything for sentimental value.

CAUTIONS

Projects go very slowly when worked on by one individual in his spare time. If the house is to be occupied immediately or at the earliest possible moment, do the necessary items at once and then plan to work in "projects" with a breather space between them. Nobody wants to live in a mess continually and nobody can work continuously without risking having the project "go sour." Be as realistic as possible. It will increase the enjoyment of doing the work and the satisfaction of the finished home. And finally, realize that your ideas may change.

Mention of a chemical in this handbook does not constitute a recommendation; only those chemicals registered by the U.S. Environmental Protection Agency may be recommended, and then only for uses as prescribed in the registration—and in the manner and at the concentration prescribed. The list of registered chemicals varies from time to time; prospective users, therefore, should get current information on registration status from Pesticides Regulation Division, Environmental Protection Agency, Washington, D.C. 20460.

Figure 13.—Exterior views of one house—before and after rehabilitation.

REHABILITATION

INTRODUCTION

This part of the handbook presents some information on materials and methods that are applicable in rehabilitating an older dwelling (fig. 13). Obviously, detailed planning cannot begin until after careful appraisal is made of the suitability of the structure for rehabilitation, as discussed in the Appraisal portion.

Our approach here is to discuss rehabilitation in a way that will be applicable to a broad range of individual interests and capabilities. Some people may be able to do the entire job of rehabilitation themselves; others may want to learn only enough so they can understand the general plan. And many in the "in-between" category may need to call for assistance in specialized areas.

In assessing the rehabilitation, what must be done, and how to do it, special assistance may be required from architects, engineers, contractors, builders, or skilled craftsmen. This could be especially true in updating critical structural items or making major structural changes. Likewise, other specialists may be required in such fields as electrical, plumbing, or heating. With the proper help, rehabilitation can be made much easier.

DEVELOPING THE PLAN

After the house has been examined and determined to be suitable for rehabilitation, plans should be made to improve the layout, provide more space, add modern conveniences, and improve appearance. Perhaps the house requires no changes and only needs restoration to its original condition, but this would be an exceptional situation. Usually changes in living patterns, conveniences, and concepts of comforts have made some remodeling desirable. Special effort and imagination should be applied toward achieving a proper layout. This increases the value of the house and gives a continuous benefit in convenience and liveability.

Before making any changes, check with the local building department, and obtain a building permit if required.

GENERAL LAYOUT

In the layout of a house it is desirable to provide separate zones for various family functions and to provide good traffic circulation through and between areas. In the moderate-cost rehabilitation project this may not be practical. Even where cost is not a major limitation, there will have to be compromises in the layout. The considerations presented here are goals to aim for where practical; inability to fully satisfy them should not prevent restoring the home to a sound, comfortable condition.

ZONED LIVING

The layout of the house should be zoned to provide three major family functional areas for relaxation, working, and privacy. The relaxation zone will include recreation, entertaining, and dining. In the small house these may all be performed in one room, but the larger house may have living room, dining room, family room or den, study, and recreation room. The latter is frequently in the basement. The working zone includes the kitchen, laundry or utility room, and may include an office or shop. The privacy zone consists of bedrooms and baths; it may include the den which can double as a guest bedroom. In some layouts a master bedroom and bath may be located away from the rest of the bedrooms so the privacy zone is actually in two parts.

Zones within the house should be located for good relationship to outdoor areas. If outdoor living in the

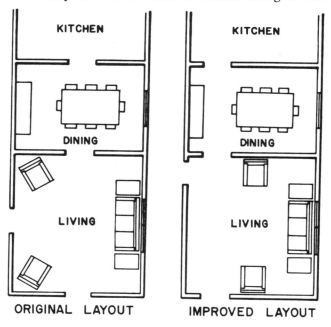

M-142 148

Figure 14.—Relocation of doors to direct traffic to one side of rooms.

16

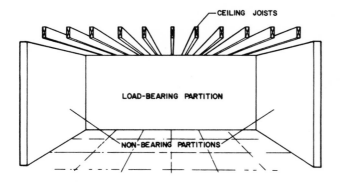

CEILING JOISTS

LOAD-BEARING PARTITION

NON-BEARING PARTITIONS

M-142 151

Figure 15.—Load-bearing and nonload-bearing partitions. (A second-floor load may place a load on any partition.)

backyard is desirable, perhaps the living room should be at the back of the house. The working zone should have good access to the garage, the dining room, and outdoor work areas. The main entrance to the house should have good access to the driveway or usual guest parking area, which may be on either the front or side of the house. In considering where to locate rooms and entrances, conventional arrangement of the past should not be binding, but convenience in the particular situation should govern.

TRAFFIC CIRCULATION

One of the most important items in layout is traffic circulation. Ideally there should be no traffic through any room. This is usually difficult to accomplish in the living and work areas. A more feasible plan is to keep traffic from cutting through the middle of the room. Many older houses have doors centered in the wall of a room; this not only directs traffic through the middle of the room, but also cuts the wall space in half, making furniture arrangement difficult. Study the plan and observe where a door might be moved from the middle of a wall space to the corner of the

room; however, movement of doors is costly and should be limited in the moderate rehabilitation job. Also consider where doors might be eliminated to prevent traffic through a room. Figure 14 shows examples of improved layout through relocation of doors.

CHANGING PARTITIONS

Often rooms are not the desired sizes, and it may be necessary to move some partitions. This is not difficult if the partition is nonload-bearing and plumbing, electrical, or heating services are not concealed in the partition. It is possible to move even load-bearing partitions by adding a beam to support the ceiling where the partition is removed.

To determine whether a partition is load bearing or not, check the span direction of ceiling joists. If joists are parallel to the partition, the partition is usually nonload-bearing (fig. 15); however, it may be supporting a second floor load so this should be checked. In most constructions where the second floor joists are perpendicular to the partition, they do require support so the partition is load-bearing (fig. 15). An exception would occur when trusses

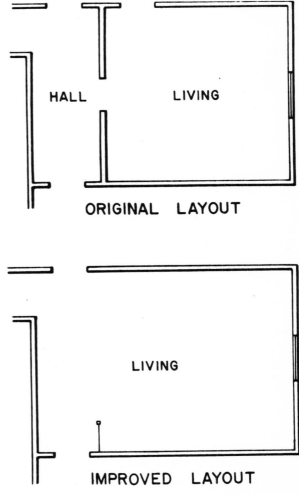

HALL

LIVING

ORIGINAL LAYOUT

LIVING

IMPROVED LAYOUT

M-142 189

Figure 17.—Removal of partition for more spacious feeling.

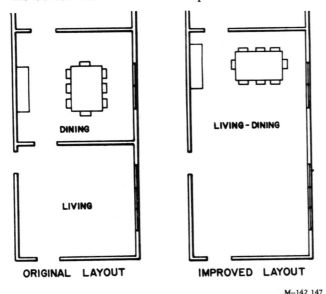

DINING

LIVING

ORIGINAL LAYOUT

LIVING-DINING

IMPROVED LAYOUT

M-142 147

Figure 16.—Removal of partition for better space utilization.

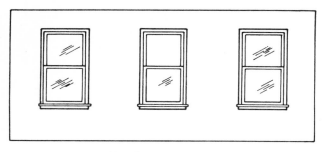

SPACED WINDOWS

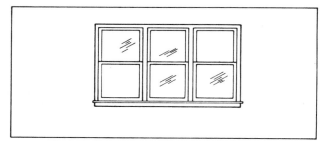

GROUPED WINDOWS

M-142 146

Figure 18.—Improved window placement through grouping.

span the width of the building, making all partitions nonload-bearing.

Although removal of a non-bearing partition will not require a structural modification, the wall, ceiling, and floor will require repairs where the partition intersected them.

If rooms are small, it may be desirable to remove partitions to give a more open spacious feeling. A partition between living and dining rooms can be removed to make both seem larger and perhaps make part of the space serve a dual purpose (fig. 16). In some instances unneeded bedrooms adjacent to the living area can be used to increase living room or other living space by removing a partition. In some rehabilitation, removing a partition between a hallway and a room in the living area gives a more spacious feeling even though traffic continues through the hallway (fig. 17).

WINDOW PLACEMENT

Windows influence general arrangement and so should also be considered in the layout. Moving windows is costly, involving changes in studs, headers, interior and exterior finish, and trim. The number of windows relocated should be very limited in the moderate-cost rehabilitation job but, where changes are practical, properly placed windows can enhance the livability of a house. Where possible, avoid small windows scattered over a wall, as they cut up the wall space and make it unusable. Attempt to group windows into one or two large areas and thus leave more wall space undisturbed (fig. 18). Where there is a choice of outside walls for window placement, south walls rank first in cold climates. Winter sun shines into the room through a south

window and heats the house, but in the summer the sun is at a higher angle so that even a small roof overhang shades the window. In extremely warm climates, north windows may be preferable to south windows to avoid heat gain even in the winter. West windows should be avoided as much as possible because the late afternoon sun is so low that there is no way of shading the window.

Windows provide three major functions: They admit daylight and sunlight, allow ventilation of the house, and provide a view. Points to consider in planning for each of these three functions are discussed below.

Some general practices to insure adequate light are:

1. Provide glass areas in excess of 10 percent of the floor area of each room.

2. Place principal window areas toward the south except in warm climates.

3. Group window openings in the wall to eliminate undesirable contrasts in brightness.

4. Screen only those parts of the window that open for ventilation.

5. Mount draperies, curtains, shades, and other window hangings above the head of the window and to the side of the window frame to free the entire glass area.

To insure good ventilation, some practices to follow are:

1. Provide ventilation in excess of 5 percent of the floor area of a room.

2. Locate the ventilation openings to take full advantage of prevailing breezes.

3. Locate windows to effect the best movement of air across the room and within the level where occupants sit or stand. (Ventilation openings should be in the lower part of the wall unless the window swings inward in a manner to direct air downward.)

To provide a good view:

1. Minimize obstructions in the line of sight for sitting or standing, depending on the use of the room.

2. Determine sill heights on the basis of room use and furniture arrangement.

CLOSETS

An item sometimes overlooked in planning the layout is closets. Most older houses have few if any closets. Plan for a coat closet near both the front and rear entrances. There should be a cleaning closet in the work area, and a linen closet in the bedroom area. Each bedroom also requires a closet. If bedrooms are large, it will be a simple matter to build a closet across one end of the room. The small house will present more difficulty. Look for waste space, such as the end of a hallway or at a wall offset. If the front door opens directly into the living room, a coat closet can sometimes be built beside or in front of the door to form an entry (fig. 19). In the story-and-a-half house, closets can often be built into the attic space where the headroom is too limited for occupancy.

Closets used for hanging clothes should ideally be at least 24 inches deep but shallower closets are also practical. Other closets can vary in depth depending on their use, but a depth greater than 24 inches is usually impractical. The exception is the walk-in storage closet, which is very useful

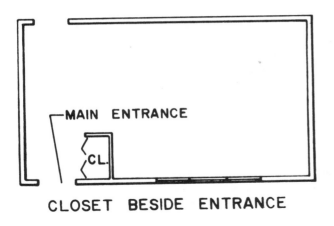

CLOSET BESIDE ENTRANCE

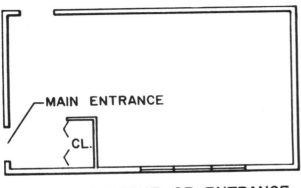

CLOSET IN FRONT OF ENTRANCE

M-142 191

Figure 19.—Entry formed by coat closet.

and should be considered if space is available. Where existing closets are narrow and deep, rollout hanging rods can make them very usable. To make the best use of closet space, plan for a full-front opening.

In many remodeling situations, plywood wardrobes may be more practical than conventional closets that require studs, drywall, casing, and doors. Very simple plywood wardrobes are illustrated in the section on closets under "Reconditioning Details." More elaborate closets can be built by dividing the wardrobe into a variety of spaces for various types of storage and installing appropriate doors or drawers.

PORCHES

Porches on older houses are often very narrow, have sloping floors, and cannot easily be enlarged. They do not lend themselves well to the type of outdoor living, such as dining and entertaining, usually desired today. Consider this in determining whether or not to retain an existing porch and in planning a new porch that will be useful.

EXPANSION WITHIN THE HOUSE

Regardless of the size of a house, there always seems to be a need for more space. Seldom is there enough storage space. Work space for a shop or other hobby area is nearly always in demand. More recreational and other informal living space are usually desired. Family rooms are seldom found in older homes. Furthermore, in some houses rooms may be small or additional bedrooms may be needed. Many older houses have only one bathroom and sometimes none, so bathroom additions are often required. Often there are possibilities for expansion by using existing unfinished space such as the attic, basement, or garage. If expansion into these areas is not practical, an addition can be built.

ATTIC

The house with a relatively steep roof slope may have some very usable attic space going to waste. It can be made accessible for storage space by the addition of a fold-down stairs. If this space is usable for living area and has an available stairway, it may be finished to form additional bedrooms, a den, a study, a hobby room, or an apartment for the relative who lives in the house but is not a member of the immediate family.

Where the attic is at third floor level, local codes should be checked. Some codes do not permit use of the third floor for living areas; others require a fire escape.

The headroom requirements for attic rooms are a minimum ceiling height of 7 feet 6 inches over at least one-half the room, and a minimum ceiling height of 5 feet at the outer edges of the room (fig. 20). The space with a lower ceiling height could be used for bunks or other built-in furniture or as storage space.

If there is sufficient headroom only in a narrow strip at the center of the attic, consider building a large shed dormer to increase the usable space (fig. 21). Dormers may be required for windows even though they are not needed for increasing space.

It is important that insulation, vapor barriers, and ventilation be considered when finishing attic space, because this space can be particularly hot in the summer. Insulate and install vapor barriers completely around walls and ceiling of the finished space and ventilate attic space above

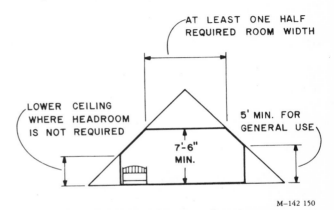

M-142 150

Figure 20.—Headroom requirements for attic rooms.

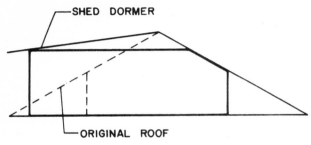

Figure 21.—Shed dormer for additional attic space.

Figure 22.—Large basement window areaway with sloped sides.

and on each side of the finished space. Provide good cross ventilation through the finished space.

An item sometimes overlooked in expanding into the attic area is a stairway. The usual straight-run stairway requires a space 3 feet wide and at least 11 feet long plus a landing at both top and bottom. There must also be a minimum overhead clearance of 6 feet 8 inches at any point on the stairs. If space is quite limited, spiral stairs may be the solution. Some spiral stairs can be installed in a space as small as 4 feet in diameter; however, code limitations should be checked. While these are quite serviceable, they are a little more difficult to ascend or descend, and so may not be suitable for the elderly. Spiral stairs will not accommodate furniture, so there must be some other access for moving furniture into the upstairs space.

BASEMENT

An unfinished basement may be one of the easiest places for expansion, although certain conditions must be met if the basement is to be used for habitable rooms. A habitable room is defined as a space used for living, sleeping, eating, or cooking. Rooms not included and, therefore, not bound by the requirements of habitable rooms include bathrooms, toilet compartments, closets, halls, storage rooms, laundry and utility rooms, and basement recreation rooms. The average finish grade elevation at exterior walls of habitable rooms should not be more than 48 inches above the finish floor. Average ceiling height for habitable rooms should be not less than 7 feet 6 inches. Local codes should be checked for exact limitations. Other basement rooms should have a minimum ceiling height of 6 feet 9 inches.

Dampness in the basement can be partially overcome by installing vapor barriers on the floor and walls if they were not installed at the time of construction. In an extremely damp basement, plan to use a dehumidifier for summer comfort.

One of the main disadvantages of basement rooms is the lack of natural light and view. If the house is on a sloping lot or graded in a manner to permit large basement windows above grade, the basement is much more usable than in the house where the basement has only a few inches of the top of the wall above grade. However, even the completely sunken basement can have natural light if large areaways are built for windows, and the walls of the areaways are sloped so that sunlight can easily reach the windows (fig. 22). At least one window large enough to serve as a fire exit is recommended and often required by

Figure 23.—Sunken garden forming large basement window areaway.

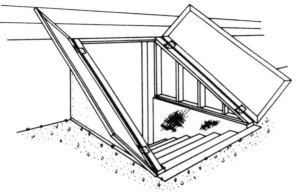

Figure 24.—Areaway type of basement entrance.

code. It may be convenient to extend the areaway to form a small sunken garden (fig. 23), but adequate drainage must be included.

The usefulness of the basement may also be increased by adding a direct outside entrance. This adds to fire safety by giving an alternate exit and is particularly desirable if the basement is to be used as a shop or for storing lawn and garden equipment. If an outside stairway is provided, try to place it under cover of a garage, breezeway, or porch to protect it from ice, snow, and rain. Otherwise, use an areaway-type entrance with a door over it (fig. 24).

GARAGE

Another place for expansion is the garage built as an integral part of the house. If the garage is well built, the only work is in finishing, which is much less costly than adding onto the house. The main consideration is whether the additional finished space is needed more than a garage. The garage is often adjacent to the kitchen, so that it is an ideal location for a large family room. It could also be used for additional bedrooms and possibly another bathroom.

Walls and ceiling of the garage can be finished in any conventional material. The floor will probably require a vapor barrier, insulation, and a new subfloor. It may be convenient to use the existing garage door opening to install large windows or a series of windows; otherwise the door opening can be completely closed and windows added at other points. Methods of adding the floor and applying other finish are presented under "Reconditioning Details."

ADDITIONS

After considering all the possibilities of expanding into the attic, basement, or garage, if space requirements are not met, the only alternative left is to construct an addition. The house on a small lot may have minimum setback limitations that will present problems. Local zoning and lot restrictions should be checked. The distance from the front of the house to the street is usually kept the same for all houses on a particular street, so expanding to the front may not be permitted. Often the house also has the minimum setback on the sides, preventing expansion on either side.

Thus, the only alternative is to add on behind the house. The house in the country usually can be expanded in any direction without restriction.

Use the addition for most critically needed space. If the need is for more bedrooms, but a much larger living room is also desirable, maybe the present living room can be used as a bedroom and a large living room can be added. If the main requirement is a large modern kitchen, add on a new kitchen and use the old kitchen as a utility room, bathroom, or some other type of living or workspace. The important thing for good appearance is that the addition be in keeping with the style of the house. Rooflines, siding, and windows should all match the original structure as closely as possible to give the house continuity, rather than giving the appearance that something has just been stuck on.

One of the most difficult problems is in connecting the addition to the original house. In some constructions it may be well to use the satellite concept, in which the addition is built as a separate building and connected to the original house by a narrow section which could serve as an entry or mudroom, and include closets or possibly a bath-

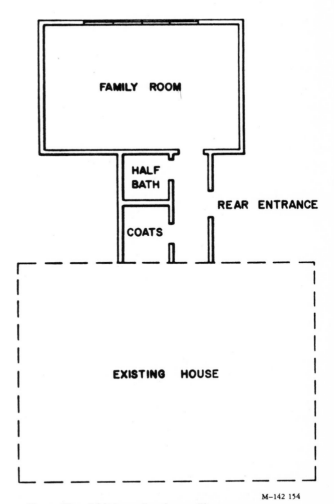

Figure 25.—Addition using the satellite concept.

21

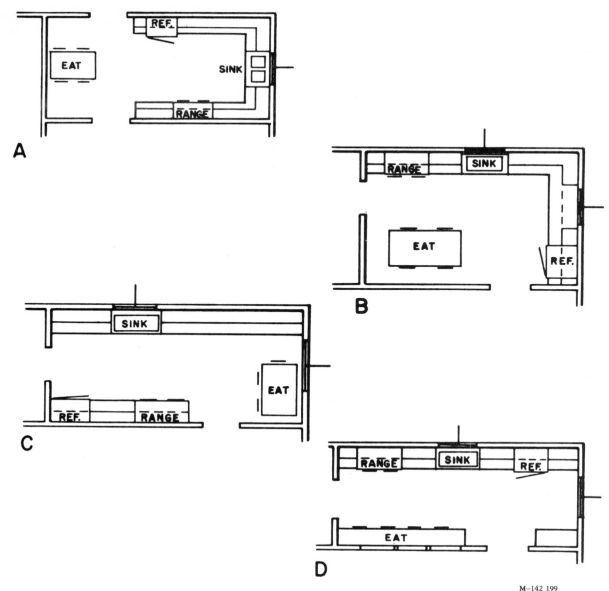

Figure 26.—Kitchen arrangements: A, U-type; B, L-type; C, corridor; D, sidewall.

M–142 199

room (fig. 25). One disadvantage of this concept is the resulting large exterior wall area with proportionate heat loss and maintenance cost for exterior surfaces.

REMODELING THE KITCHEN

New appliances and present concepts of convenience have revolutionized the kitchen in recent years. More space is required for the numerous appliances now considered necessary.

In spite of changing requirements, some principles of kitchen planning have applied for several years. The basic movements in food preparation are from the refrigerator to the sink, and then to the range. The four generally recognized arrangements for kitchens are: the "U" and "L" types, corridor, and sidewall (fig. 26). The arrangement selected depends on the amount of space, the shape of the space, and the location of doors. If the kitchen is going to be a new addition, select the layout preferred, and plan the addition in accordance with the layout. The work triangle is smallest in the "U" and corridor layouts. The sidewall arrangement is preferred where space is quite limited, and the "L" arrangement is used in a relatively square kitchen that must have a dining table in it.

If kitchen cabinet space is adequate and well arranged, updating the cabinets may be the only desirable change. New doors and drawer fronts can be added to the old cabinet framing. Even refinishing or painting the old cabinets and adding new hardware can sometimes do much to improve an old kitchen. If a kitchen has adequate cabinets, the single improvement that will most update it is new counter tops. Tops should be fabricated and installed by a good custom counter shop. Plastic laminate over particleboard backing is commonly used.

22

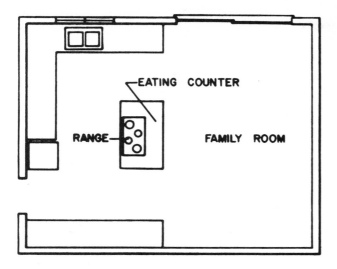

Figure 27.—Island counter dividing kitchen and family room.

Doorways should be located to avoid traffic through the work triangle. Generally doorways in corners should be avoided, and door swings should avoid conflict with the use of appliances, cabinets, or other doors. If swinging the door out would put it in the path of travel in a hall or other activity area, consider using a sliding or folding door. Sliding doors and installation are expensive, but may be worth the expense in certain situations.

Windows should be adequate to make the kitchen a light cheerful place, because the homemaker spends much of her time there. The current trend toward indoor-outdoor living has fostered the "patio kitchen," with large windows over a counter which extends to the outside to provide an outdoor eating counter. This is particularly useful in the warmer climates, but also convenient for summer use in any climate.

The placement of the sink in relation to windows is a matter of personal preference. Many women like to look out the window while they are at the sink, but installing the sink along an interior plumbing partition is usually less costly than on an outside wall.

If the kitchen is quite large, it may be convenient to use part as a family room. The combined kitchen-family room concept can also be met by removing a partition to expand the kitchen or by adding on a large room. One method of arranging workspace conveniently in such a room is by using an island counter (fig. 27), which can also serve as an eating counter for informal dining.

Much research in kitchen planning has been done by the U.S. Department of Agriculture's Agricultural Research Service and by State universities. Contact the local Agriculture Extension Service for bulletins on kitchen planning from these sources. Many companies building kitchen cabinets will also assist in planning.

ADDING A BATH

Improved bathroom facilities should be one of the main considerations in the planning stages of remodeling. There should be plans to add a bath where there is none, and a half bath or second bath should be considered for many houses with only one bath.

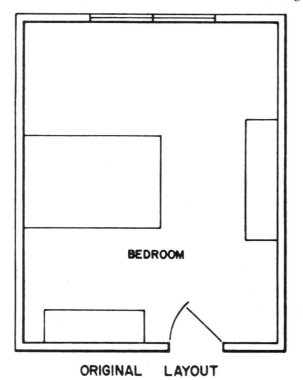

ORIGINAL LAYOUT

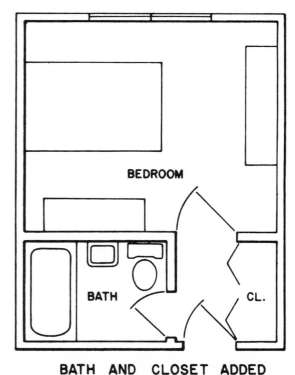

BATH AND CLOSET ADDED

Figure 28.—Portion of a large bedroom used to add a bath.

23

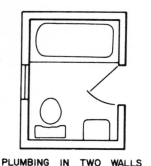
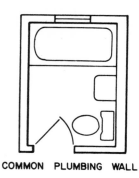

PLUMBING IN TWO WALLS   COMMON PLUMBING WALL

M-142 149

Figure 29.—Minimum size bathroom (5 ft by 7 ft).

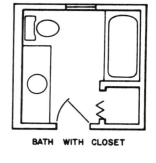
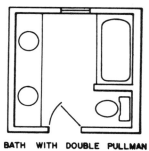

BATH WITH CLOSET   BATH WITH DOUBLE PULLMAN

M-142 157

Figure 30.—Moderate size bathroom (8 ft by 8 ft).

Finding a convenient location to add a bath in an existing house is often quite difficult. Adding a room onto the house is seldom a good solution because it is usually desirable to have access to the bath from a bedroom hallway. A half bath near the main entrance or in the work area is desirable. One consideration in locating a bath economically is to keep all piping runs as short as possible. Also, all fixtures on one plumbing wall can use a common vent.

One prevalent mistake in adding a bath in an older house has been to place it in any unused space without regard to convenience of location. Consequently, many bathrooms have been placed in what was formerly a pantry, a large closet, or under a stairway. This usually means the only access to the bathroom is through the kitchen or a bedroom, or that the bathroom is totally removed from the bedroom area. If this mistake has been made in a house, it is important to add another bath in a good location.

In a house with large bedrooms, a portion of one bedroom can be taken for a bath (fig. 28). Such a bedroom should be at least 16 feet in one dimension so that it will still be no less than 10 feet in least dimension after the bath is built. If the bedrooms are small and all are needed, there may be no choice except to build an addition. It may be advantageous to make a small bedroom into a bath (or two baths) and add on another bedroom. A possibility in the one-and-one-half-story house is to add a bath in the area under the shed dormer (fig. 21). When this is done,

remember that the wall containing the plumbing must have a wall below it on the first floor through which piping can run. This applies to two-story houses also.

The minimum size for a bathroom is 5 feet by 7 feet (fig. 29), and larger sizes are certainly desirable. Increasing the size slightly would make the bath less cramped and could provide space for a storage closet for towels, cleaning equipment, or supplies (fig. 30). If the plan is for only one bath, consider making it in compartments for use by more than one person at a time (fig. 31). Two baths can be most economically built with fixtures back to back (fig. 32), but do not sacrifice convenience of location to accomplish this. Bathrooms built on both floors of a two-story house are most economically built with second floor bath directly over the first floor bath.

Bathroom fixtures vary in size, so fixture dimensions from the building supply dealer are required to make detailed plans. Minimum dimensions between and around fixtures are shown in figure 33.

APPEARANCE

Many older houses possess desirable qualities of appearance that should be retained. Many new house designs copy styles of the past in an attempt to capture the dignity of the two-story Colonial, the quaintness of the Victorian house, the charm of the old English cottage, the look of solid comfort of the Midwestern farmhouse, or the rustic infor-

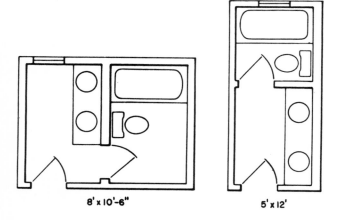

8' x 10'-6"   5' x 12'

M-142 158

Figure 31.—Compartmented bathroom.

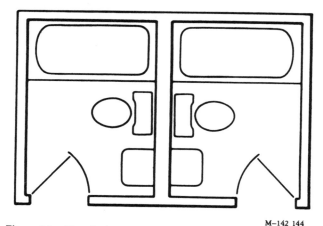

M-142 144

Figure 32.—Two bathrooms with economical back-to-back arrangement.

24

mality of the ranch house. If a house possesses any of these or other desirable qualities, it may be well to avoid any change of appearance. To retain the character of the house, all additions, new windows and doors and covering materials, must be in keeping with the existing character.

When changes in appearance are planned, two key elements that should be foremost are unity and simplicity. To achieve unity, make rooflines continuous where possible, make all windows the same type and use only one or two siding materials. Avoid trim that appears stuck onto the house without serving any purpose, and remove such trim where it does exist. The result is not only simplicity, but also a reduction in maintenance costs. An exception to this treatment of trim is the good period style in which added maintenance may be justified in preserving the character of the home. In two-story houses windows are generally lined up and placed over each other on a first and second floor. Relocation of a window on either floor could destroy the unity and simplicity of the house.

One of the most common causes of poor appearance is a lack of roof overhang (fig. 34). There should be a roof overhang of at least 1 foot and preferably 2 feet all around the house to protect the siding and windows as well as to give a good appearance. If this overhang is lacking, consider adding an overhang during the remodeling. It should pay for itself in reduced maintenance in addition to improving the appearance of the house.

For the house that is exceptionally plain, one of the best places to add interest is at the main entrance. This is the natural focal point for the house and an attractive door, a raised planter, or interesting steps can do much to enhance overall appearance. One caution is to keep the entrance in scale and in character with the house, and to avoid an overly grand appearance.

The house that looks too tall can often be improved by adding strong horizontal lines as porch or carport roofs. Painting the first and second story different colors can also produce a lower appearance. Color can also affect the appar-

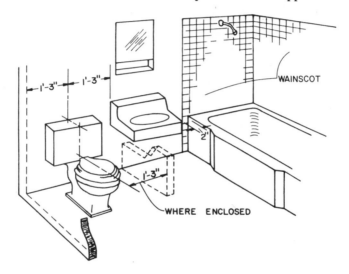

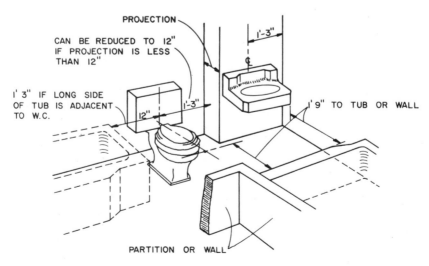

M-142 160

Figure 33.—Recommended dimensions for fixture spacing.

25

A

B

M-142 188

Figure 34.—Improved appearance by adding roof overhang: A,
without overhang; B, with overhang.

ent size of the house. A light color makes a house appear large whereas a dark color will make it appear much smaller.

Interior appearance should also be considered before finish materials are selected. The most convenient materials to apply do not always produce the desired character. Ceiling tile that is attractive in a recreation room may not be suitable in a living room. Paneling comes in various types and qualities which also result in major differences in the dignity and charm of a room. Keep the desired effect in mind as plans are made.

RECONDITIONING DETAILS

With the information from a thorough examination of the house and a complete plan for changes to be made, the actual rehabilitation can begin. In locations where termites are a particular problem (fig. 35), and are prevalent in and around the house, soil poisoning may be advisable before the work begins. Local information on termites may be available from the County Extension Office.

The order in which components of the house are reconditioned will vary with each situation; however, the first step in rehabilitation should be to level the house and floor system. A level base to work from is essential to a good rehabilitation job. Roof repairs and changes in windows and exterior doors should be made before interior work begins. All changes in plumbing, electrical wiring, and heating should also be completed before interior finish work is started.

Certain general information will be useful in reconditioning wood-frame construction:

(1) Moisture content of framing material should not exceed 19 percent, and a maximum of 15 percent would be better in most areas of the United States.

(2) Recommended moisture content for interior finish woodwork varies from 6 to 11 percent depending on the area of the United States. A map showing recommended average moisture contents is shown in figure 36.

(3) Plywood should be exterior type anywhere it will be exposed to moisture during construction or in use.

(4) Recommended nailing for assembly of framing and application of covering materials is listed in table 1. Sizes of common nails are shown in figure 37.

(5) Actual lumber sizes have changed and new lumber may not be fully compatible with that of old framing. Some older homes may have been constructed using full thickness lumber, so allowance must be made for size differences.

BASIC STRUCTURE

FOUNDATION

Because a relatively good foundation is a prime requisite of a house worth rehabilitating, no major repairs or replacement will be discussed.

Soil Poisoning Around Foundation

Subterranean termites are the only wood-destroying insects that may require measures beyond those provided by sound construction practices. Generally, the most widely recommended form of supplementary treatment against the termites is soil poisoning. The treatment also is an effective remedial measure.

Studies made by the U.S. Department of Agriculture show that certain chemicals added to soil under buildings or around foundations will prevent or control termite infestation for many years.[2] Generally such treatments will be applied by a professional exterminator.

Slab construction.—The treatment of soil under slab-on-ground construction is difficult. One method of treatment consists of drilling holes about a foot apart through the concrete slab, adjacent to all cracks and expansion joints, and injecting a chemical into the soil beneath the slab. Another method is to drill through the perimeter foundation walls from the outside and force the chemical just beneath the slab along the inside of the foundation and along all cracks and expansion joints.

Crawl-space houses.—To treat buildings having crawl spaces, dig trenches adjacent to and around all piers and pipes and along the sides of foundation walls (fig. 38). Around solid concrete foundations the trenches should be 6 to 8 inches deep and wide. Chemical is poured into the trench and, as the excavated soil is put back into the trench, it also is treated. The soil is tamped, and the trench

---

[2] Specific chemicals to be used for control should be those registered by the Environmental Protection Agency, and then only for uses as prescribed in the registration, and in the manner and concentration prescribed. Because the list of registered chemicals varies from time to time, prospective users should get current information from the Environmental Protection Agency, Washington, D.C.

M–134 686

Figure 35.—The northern limit of damage in the United States by subterranean termites, line A; by dry-wood or nonsubterranean termites, line B.

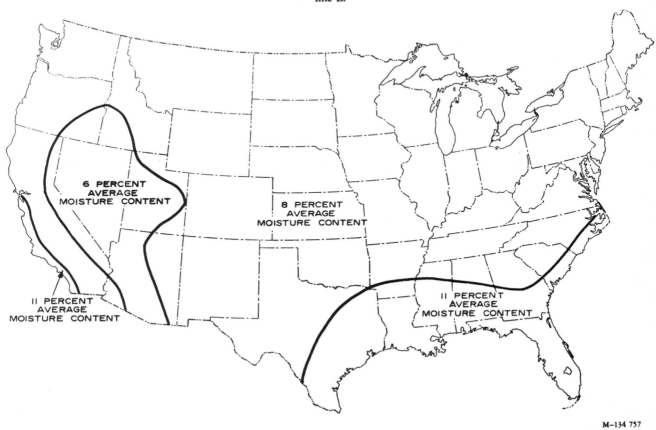

M–134 757

Figure 36.—Recommended average moisture content for interior finish woodwork in different parts of the United States.

Table 1.—*Recommended schedule for nailing the framing and sheathing of a well-constructed wood-frame house*

Joining	Nailing method	Nails		
		Number	Size	Placement
Header to joist	End nail	3	16d	—
Joist to sill or girder	Toenail	2	10d	—
			or 8d	
Header and stringer joist to sill	Toenail	—	10d	16 in. on center
Bridging to joist	Toenail each end	2	8d	—
Ledger strip to beam, 2 in. thick	—	3	16d	At each joist
Subfloor, boards:				
1 by 6 in. and smaller	—	2	8d	To each joist
1 by 8 in.	—	3	8d	To each joist
Subfloor, plywood:				
At edges	—	—	8d	6 in. on center
At intermediate joists	—	—	8d	8 in. on center
Subfloor (2 by 6 in., T&G) to joist or girder	Blind nail (casing) and face nail	2	16d	
Soleplate to stud, horizontal assembly	End nail	2	16d	At each stud
Top plate to stud	End nail	2	16d	
Stud to soleplate	Toenail	4	8d	—
Soleplate to joist or blocking	Face nail	—	16d	16 in. on center
Doubled studs	Face nail, stagger	—	10d	16 in. on center
End stud of intersecting wall to exterior wall stud	Face nail	—	16d	16 in. on center
Upper top plate to lower top plate	Face nail	—	16d	16 in. on center
Upper top plate, laps and intersections	Face nail	2	16d	—
Continuous header, two pieces, each edge	—	—	12d	12 in. on center
Ceiling joist to top wall plates	Toenail	3	8d	—
Ceiling joist laps at partition	Face nail	4	16d	—
Rafter to top plate	Toenail	2	8d	—
Rafter to ceiling joist	Face nail	5	10d	—
Rafter to valley or hip rafter	Toenail	3	10d	—
Ridge board to rafter	End nail	3	10d	—
Rafter to rafter through ridge board	Toenail	4	8d	—
	Edge nail	1	10d	—
Collar beam to rafter:				
2-in. member	Face nail	2	12d	—
1-in. member	Face nail	3	8d	—
1-in. diagonal let-in brace to each stud and plate (four nails at top)	—	2	8d	
Built-up corner studs:				
Studs to blocking	Face nail	2	10d	Each side
Intersecting stud to corner studs	Face nail	—	16d	12 in. on center
Built-up girders and beams, three or more members	Face nail	—	20d	32 in. on center, each side
Wall sheathing:				
1 by 8 in. or less, horizontal	Face nail	2	8d	At each stud
1 by 6 in. or greater, diagonal	Face nail	3	8d	At each stud
Wall sheathing, vertically applied plywood:				
3/8 in. and less thick	Face nail	—	6d	6-in. edge and 12-in. intermediate
1/2 in. and over thick	Face nail	—	8d	
Wall sheathing, vertically applied fiberboard:				
1/2 in. thick	Face nail	—	(1)	3-in. edge and 6-in. intermediate
25/32 in. thick	Face nail	—	(2)	
Roof sheathing, board, 4-, 6-, 8-in. width	Face nail	2	8d	At each rafter
Roof sheathing, plywood:				
3/8 in. and less thick	Face nail	—	6d	6-in. edge and 12-in. intermediate
1/2 in. and over thick	Face nail	—	8d	

[1] 1 1/2-in. roofing nail.
[2] 1 3/4-in. roofing nail.

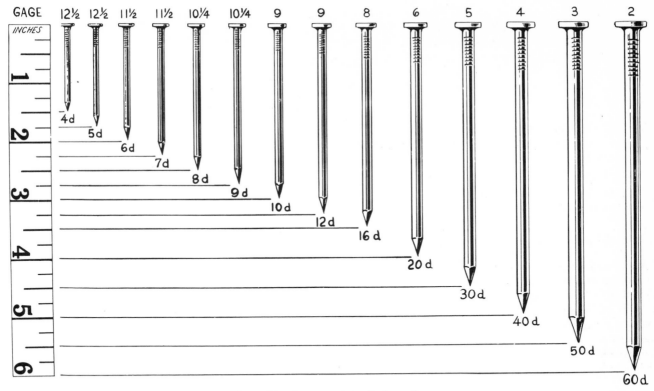

Figure 37.—Common sizes of wire nails.

ZM–681 69F

filled to a level above the surrounding soil to provide good drainage away from the foundation.

In brick, hollow-block, or concrete foundations that have cracked, dig the trench to, but not below, the footing. Then as the trench is refilled, treat the soil. Treat voids in hollow-block foundations by applying the chemical to the voids at or near the footing.

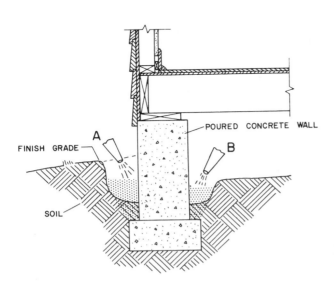

M–142 192

Figure 38.—Application of chemical to crawl-space construction soil treatment: A, along outside wall; and B, inside foundation wall.

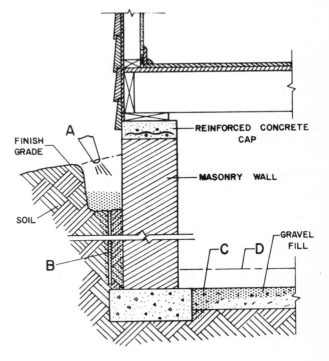

M–142 193

Figure 39.—Application of chemical to the soil in and around a full basement: A, soil treatment along outside of the foundation; B, pipe and rod hole from bottom of trench to the top of the footing to aid distribution of the chemical; C, drill holes for the treatment of fill or soil beneath a concrete floor in basement; D, position of concrete slab.

Basement houses.—Application of soil poisoning for this type of construction is much the same as for slab-on-ground and crawl-space construction (fig. 39). Treat the basement floor in the same way as a slab-on-ground house.

Precautions.—Chemicals for termite control are poisonous to people and animals. Be sure to use them properly and safely. Here are some basic safety rules:

Carefully read all labels and follow directions.
Store insecticides in labeled containers out of reach of children and animals.

Dispose of empty containers.
Wash contaminated parts of body with warm, soapy water immediately after exposure.

Cracks in Concrete Foundation

Minor hairline cracks frequently occur in concrete walls during its curing process and usually require no repair. Open cracks should be repaired, but the type of repair depends on whether the crack is active or dormant and whether waterproofing is necessary. One of the simplest methods of determining if the crack is active is to place a mark at each end of the crack and observe at future dates whether the crack extends beyond the marks.

If the crack is dormant, it can be repaired by routing and sealing. Routing is accomplished by following along the crack with a concrete saw or chipping with hand tools to enlarge the crack near the concrete surface. The crack is first routed $1/4$ inch or more in width and about the same depth; then the routed joint is rinsed clean and allowed to dry. A joint sealer such as an epoxy-cement compound should then be applied in accordance with manufacturer's instructions.

Working cracks require an elastic sealant. These should also be applied in accordance with manufacturer's instructions. Sealants vary greatly in elasticity, so a good-quality sealant that will remain pliable should be used. The minimum depth of routing for these sealants is $3/4$ to 1 inch, and the width is about the same. The elastic material can then deform with movement of the crack. Strip sealants which can be applied to the surface are also available, but these protrude from the surface and may be objectionable.

Crumbling Mortar

Where masonry foundations or piers have crumbling mortar joints, these should be repaired. First chip out all loose mortar and brush thoroughly to remove all dust and loose particles. Before applying new mortar, dampen the clean surface so that it will not absorb water from the mixture. Mortar can be purchased premixed. It should have about the consistency of putty and should be applied like a calking material. For a good bond, force the mortar into the crack to contact all depressions. Then smooth the surface with a trowel. Provide some protection from sun and wind for a few days to keep the mortar from drying out too fast.

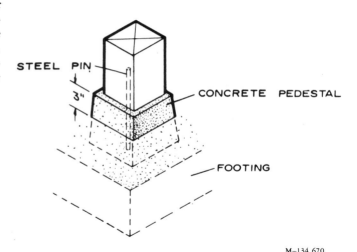

STEEL PIN

3"

CONCRETE PEDESTAL

FOOTING

M–134 670

Figure 40.—Basement post on pedestal above the floor.

Uneven Settlement

Uneven settlement in a concrete foundation due to poor footings or no footings at all usually damages the foundation to the point that precludes repair. In a pier foundation the individual pier or piers could be replaced or, if the pier has stopped settling, blocking could be added on top of the pier to level the house. In either situation, the girder or joists being supported must be jacked and held in a level position while the repairs are being made.

Basement Posts

Any type of basement post may have settled due to inadequate footings, or wood posts may have deteriorated due to decay or insect damage. To correct either problem, a well-supported jack must be used to raise the floor girder off the post in question. This releveling must be done slowly and carefully to avoid cracking the plaster in the house walls. Steel jack posts are convenient replacements for the post removed. If a wood post is used, a pedestal should be built to raise the base of the post slightly above the floor surface (fig. 40). This allows the end of the post to dry out if it becomes wet.

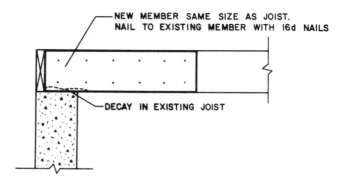

NEW MEMBER SAME SIZE AS JOIST.
NAIL TO EXISTING MEMBER WITH 16d NAILS

DECAY IN EXISTING JOIST

M–142 159

Figure 41.—Repair of joist with decay in end contacting the foundation.

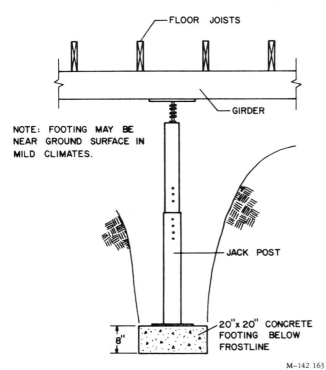

FLOOR JOISTS

GIRDER

NOTE: FOOTING MAY BE NEAR GROUND SURFACE IN MILD CLIMATES.

JACK POST

8"

20"x 20" CONCRETE FOOTING BELOW FROSTLINE

M–142 163

Figure 42.—Jack post supporting a sagging girder in a crawl-space house.

FLOOR SYSTEM

Replacement of Framing Members

If examination of the floor framing revealed decay or insect damage in a limited number of framing members, the members affected will have to be replaced or the affected sections repaired. Large-scale damage would probably have resulted in classifying the house as not worth rehabilitation. Damaged members should be replaced with preservative treated wood if exposure conditions are severe. To accomplish this, the framing supported by the damaged member must be temporarily supported by jacks in a crawl-space house or jacks with blocking in a basement house. A heavy crossarm on top of the jack will support a width of house of 4 to 6 feet. Where additional support is necessary, more jacks are required. Raise the jacks carefully and

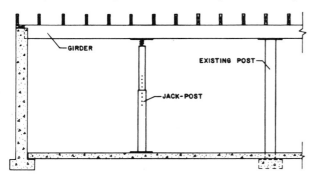

GIRDER

EXISTING POST

JACK-POST

M–142 162

Figure 43.—Jack post used to level a sagging girder in a basement house.

slowly, and only enough to take the weight off the member to be removed. Excessive jacking will pull the building frame out of square. After the new or repaired member is in place, gradually take the weight off the jack and remove it.

Sometimes decay may exist in only a small part of a member. An example might be the end of a floor joist supported on a concrete foundation wall; it could contain decay only where the wood contacts the concrete. After applying a brushed-on preservative to the affected area, jack the existing joist into place and nail a short length of new material to the side of the joist (fig. 41).

Leveling the Floor

After the foundation repairs have been properly made, the support points for the floor should be level; however, the floor may still sag. Where the floor joists have sagged excessively, permanent set may have occurred and little can be done except by replacement of the floor joists. A slight sag can be overcome by nailing a new joist alongside alternate joists in the affected area. If the new joists are slightly bowed, place them crown up. Each joist must be jacked at both ends to force the ends to the same elevation as the existing joist. The same treatment can be used to stiffen springy floors.

Girders that sag excessively should be replaced. Excessive set cannot be removed. Jack posts can be used to level slightly sagged girders or to install intermediate girders, but unless the space is little used or jack posts can be incorporated into a wall, they are generally in the way. Methods for installing jack posts are shown in figures 42 and 43.

When jack posts are used to stiffen a springy floor or to carry light loads, they can be set directly on the concrete floor slab. Where they are used to support heavy loads, a steel plate may be necessary to distribute the load over a larger area of the floor slab. The jack post should not be used for heavy jacking. Where heavy jacking is involved, use a regular jack to carefully lift the load, and then put the jack post in place.

Elimination of Squeaks

Squeaks in flooring frequently are caused by relative movement of the tongue of one flooring strip in the groove of the adjacent strip. One of the simplest remedies is to apply a limited amount of mineral oil to the joints.

Sagging floor joists often pull away from the subfloor and result in excessive deflection of the floor. If this is the cause of squeaks, squeeze construction mastic into the open joints. An alternate remedy is to drive small wedges into the spaces between joists and subfloor (fig. 44). Drive them only far enough for a snug fit. This method of repair should be limited to a small area.

Undersized floor joists that deflect excessively are also a major cause of squeaks. The addition of girders (described previously) to shorten the joist span is the best solution to that problem.

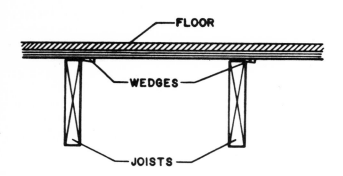

Figure 44.—Wedges driven between joists and subfloor to stop squeaks.

M–142 161

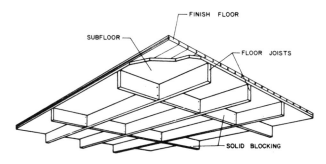

Figure 45.—Solid blocking between floor joists where finish floor is laid parallel to joists.

M–142 142

Strip flooring installed parallel to the joists may also deflect excessively. Solid blocking nailed between joists and fitted snugly against the subfloor (fig. 45) will prevent this deflection if installed at relatively close spacing.

One of the most common causes of squeaking is inadequate nailing. To correct this, drive a nail through the face of the flooring board near the tongue edge into the subfloor—preferably also into a joist. Set the nail and fill the hole. A less objectionable method from the standpoint of appearance is to work from under the floor using screws driven through the subfloor into the finish floor. This method will also bring warped flooring into a flat position.

New Floor Covering

Floor covering is available in a variety of materials. These include wood in various forms; asphalt, vinyl, vinyl asbestos, rubber, and cork tile; ceramics; linoleum; sheet vinyl; carpeting; and liquid seamless flooring. The material selected depends on existing conditions, the planned use of the floor, and the homeowner's budget.

Before any floor is laid, a suitable base must be prepared. Unless existing wood flooring is exceptionally smooth, it should receive a light sanding to remove irregularities before any covering is put over it. If a thin underlayment or no underlayment is being used, wide joints between floor boards should be filled to avoid showthrough on the less rigid types of finish floor. An underlayment of plywood or wood-base panel material installed over the old floor is required when linoleum or resilient tile is used for the new finish floor.

Where underlayment is required, it should be in 4– by 4–foot or larger sheets of untempered hardboard, plywood, or particleboard $1/4$ or $3/8$ inches thick. Some floor coverings are not guaranteed over all types of underlayments, so check the manufacturers' recommendations before choosing an underlayment. Underlayment grade of plywood has a sanded, C–plugged or Better face ply and a C–ply or Better immediately under the face. It is available in interior types, exterior types, and interior types with exterior glue. The interior type is generally adequate but one of the other two types should be used where there is possible exposure to moisture. Underlayment should be laid with $1/32$–inch edge and end spacing to allow for expansion. Nail the underlayment to the subfloor using the type of nail and spacing recommended by the underlayment manufacturer.

Installation over existing flooring.—Wood flooring, sheet vinyl with resilient backing, seamless flooring, and carpeting can all be installed directly over the old flooring after major voids have been filled and it has been sanded

Table 2.—*Grade and description of strip flooring of several species and grain orientation*

Species	Grain orientation	Size		First grade	Second grade	Third grade
		Thickness	Face width			
		In.	*In.*			
		SOFTWOODS				
Douglas-fir and hemlock	Edge grain	25/32	2 3/8–5 3/16	B and Better	C	D
	Flat grain	25/32	2 3/8–5 3/16	C and Better	D	—
Southern pine	Edge grain	5/16–	1 3/4–5 7/16	B and Better	C and Better	D (and No. 2)
	Flat grain	1 5/16				
		HARDWOODS				
Oak	Edge grain	25/32	1 1/2–3 1/4	Clear	Select	
	Flat grain	3/8	1 1/2, 2	Clear	Select	No. 1 Common
		1/2	1 1/2, 2			
Beech, birch, maple, and pecan[1]		25/32	1 1/2–3 1/4	First grade	Second grade	
		3/8	1 1/2, 2			
		1/2	1 1/2, 2			

[1] Special grades are available in which uniformity of color is a requirement.

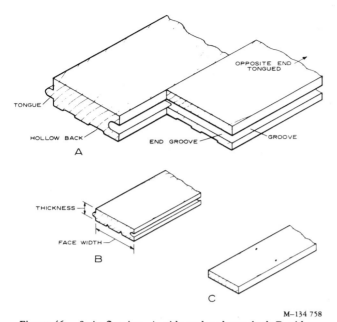

Figure 46.—Strip flooring, A, side and end matched; B, side matched; C, square edged.

relatively smooth. These coverings can also be installed over old resilient tile which is still firmly cemented.

Wood flooring may be hardwood or softwood. Grades and descriptions are listed in table 2. Types are illustrated in figure 46.

Hardwood flooring is available in strip or block and is usually tongued and grooved and end matched, but it may be square-edged in thinner patterns. The most widely used pattern of hardwood strip flooring is $25/32$ by $2\frac{1}{4}$ inches with hollow back. Strips are random lengths varying from 2 to 16 feet long. The face is slightly wider than the bottom so that tight joints result.

Softwood flooring is also available in strip or block. Strip flooring has tongued-and-grooved edges, and some types are also end matched. Softwood flooring costs less than

most hardwood species, but is less wear-resistant and shows surface abrasions more readily. However, it can be used in light traffic areas.

Bundles of flooring should be broken and kept in a heated space until the moisture content common to interior finish in the locale is achieved (fig. 36).

Strip flooring is normally laid crosswise to the floor joists; however, when laid over old strip flooring, it should be laid crosswise to the existing flooring. Nail sizes and types vary with the thickness of the flooring. For $25/32$-inch flooring use eightpenny flooring nails; use sixpenny flooring nails for $1/2$-inch flooring; and use fourpenny casing nails for $3/8$-inch flooring. Other nails, such as the ring-shank and screw-shank types, can be used, but it is well to check the flooring manufacturer's recommendations on size and diameter for specific uses. Flooring brads with blunted points which prevent splitting of the tongue are also available.

Begin installing matched flooring by placing the first strip $1/2$ to $5/8$ inch away from the wall to allow for expansion when the moisture content increases. Nail straight down through the board near the grooved edge (fig. 47). The nail should be close enough to the wall to be covered by the base or shoe molding and should be driven into a joist when the flooring is laid crosswise to the joists. The tongue should also be nailed, and consecutive flooring boards should be nailed through the tongue only. Nails are driven into the tongue at an angle of 45° to 50° and are not driven quite flush, to prevent damaging the edge by the hammer head (fig. 48). The nail is then set with the end of a large nail set or by laying the nail set flatwise against the flooring. Contractors use nailing devices designed especially for nailing flooring. These drive and set the nail in one operation.

Select lengths of flooring boards so that butts will be well separated in adjacent courses. Drive each board tightly against the one previously installed. Crooked boards should

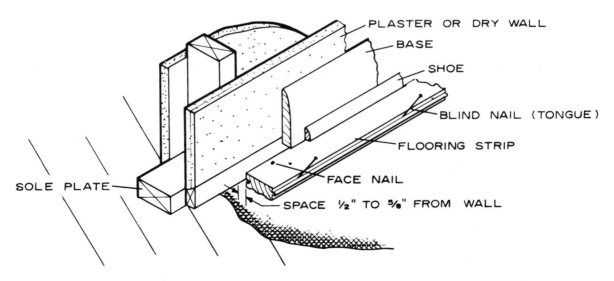

Figure 47.—Installation of first strip of flooring.

33

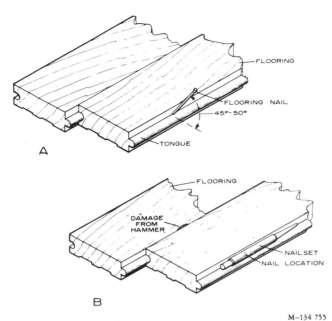

Figure 48.—Nailing of flooring; A, angle of nailing; B, setting the nail without damage to the flooring.

be forced into alinement or cut off and used at the ends of a course or in closets.

The last course of flooring should be left $\frac{1}{2}$ to $\frac{5}{8}$ inch from the wall, just as the first course was. Face-nail it near the edge where the base or shoe will cover the nail.

Square-edged strip flooring must be installed over a substantial subfloor and can only be face-nailed. The installation procedures relative to spacing at walls, spacing of joints, and general attachment are the same as those for matched flooring.

Most wood or wood-base tile is applied with an adhesive to a smooth base such as underlayment or a finished concrete floor with a properly installed vapor barrier. Wood tile may be made up of a number of narrow slats held together by a membrane, cleats, or tape to form a square, or it may be plywood with tongued-and-grooved edges (fig. 49). To install wood tile, an adhesive is spread on the concrete slab or underlayment with a notched trowel, and the tile laid in it. Follow the manufacturer's recommendation for adhesive and method of application.

Wood block flooring may have tongues on two edges and grooves in the other two edges and is usually nailed through the tongue into a wood subfloor. It may be applied on concrete with the use of an adhesive. Shrinkage and swelling effects of wood block flooring are minimized by changing the grain direction of alternate blocks.

Particleboard tile is installed in much the same manner as wood tile, except it should not be used over concrete. Manufacturer's instructions for installation are usually quite complete. This tile is usually 9 by 9 by $\frac{3}{8}$ inches in size, with tongued-and-grooved edges. The back is often marked with small saw kerfs to stabilize the tile and provide a better key for the adhesive.

Sheet vinyl with resilient backing smooths out minor surface imperfections. Most vinyl will lay flat, so no adhesive is required. Double-faced tape is used at joints and around the edge to keep the covering from moving. Most sheet vinyls are available in widths of 6, 9, 12, and 15 feet, so that complete rooms can be covered with a minimum of splicing. This permits a fast, easy installation. The material is merely cut to room size, using scissors, and is then taped down.

Seamless flooring consisting of resin chips combined with a urethane binder can be applied over any stable base, including old floor tile. This is applied as a liquid in several coats with drying between coats. Complete application may take from $\frac{1}{2}$ to 2 days depending on the brand used. Manufacturer's instructions for application are quite complete. This floor covering is easily renewed by additional coatings, and damaged spots are easily patched by adding more chips and binder.

Carpeting also lends itself well to rehabilitation. It can be installed over almost any flooring that is level, relatively smooth, and free from major surface imperfections. Carpeting is now available for all rooms in the house, including the kitchen. A very close weave is used for kitchen carpeting so that spills stay on the surface and are easily wiped up. The cost of carpeting may be two or three times that of a finished wood floor, and the life of the carpeting before replacement would be much less than that of a wood floor. However, carpeting requires less maintenance and has the advantages of sound-absorption and resistance to impact.

Installation over underlayment.—Linoleum and resilient tile both require a smooth underlayment or a smooth concrete slab to which they are bonded with an adhesive. Linoleum should not be laid on concrete slabs on the ground or basement floors, but many of the resilient tiles can be used.

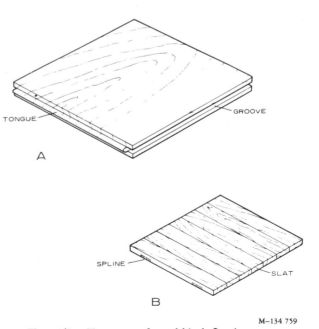

Figure 49.—Two types of wood block flooring.

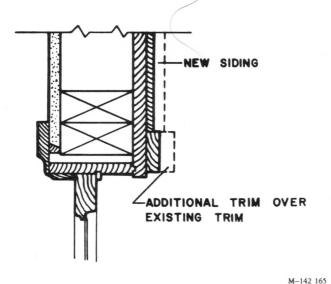

M-142 165

Figure 50.—Top view of window casing extended by adding trim over existing trim.

Linoleum is available in a variety of thicknesses and grades and is usually in 6–foot–wide rolls. It is laid in accordance with manufacturer's directions, and usually rolled to insure adhesion to the floor.

One of the lower cost resilient coverings is asphalt tile. Some types are damaged by grease and oil, and so should not be used in kitchens. This tile is about $1/8$ inch thick and either 9 or 12 by 12 inches in size. Adhesive for this tile is spread using a notched trowel, with both size of notches and adhesive recommended by the manufacturer.

Other types of tile, such as vinyl, vinyl-asbestos, rubber, and cork, are also usually available in 9– by 9– or 12– by 12–inch size but are sometimes larger. It is important that

all these tile be laid so the joints do not coincide with the joints of the underlayment. The manufacturer's directions usually include instructions on laying baselines near the center of the room and parallel to its length and width. The baselines are then used as a starting point in laying the tile.

Siding

The solution for wood siding problems often involves corrective measures in other components of the house. Failure of paint is frequently not the fault of the siding but can be attributed to moisture moving out through the wall or to water washing down the face of the wall. Corrective measures are discussed under sections on "Vapor Barriers" and "Roof System." After adopting these corrective measures, siding may need only refinishing as discussed in the section on "Painting and Finishing." Some of the "permanent" sidings that require no painting may cause serious difficulty in time by trapping moisture in the wall, thus creating a decay hazard. It is desirable, therefore, to have a siding that will let water vapor escape from inside the wall.

If new horizontal wood or nonwood siding is used, it will probably be best to remove old siding. Vertical board and panel-type siding may be successfully applied over old siding.

The main difficulty in applying new siding over existing siding is in adjusting the window and door trim to compensate for the added wall thickness. The window sills on most houses extend far enough beyond the siding so that new siding should not affect them; however, the casing may be nearly flush with the siding and require some type of extension. One method of extending the casing is by adding an additional trim member over the existing casing (fig. 50). When this is done, a wider drip cap may also be required. The drip cap could be replaced, or it could be reused with blocking behind it to hold it out from the wall a distance equal to the new siding thickness (fig. 51).

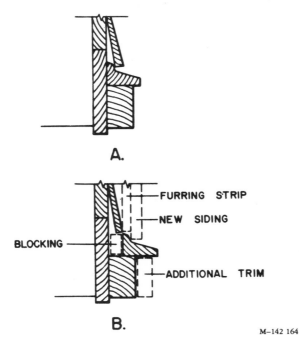

M-142 164

Figure 51.—Change in drip cap with new siding: A, existing drip cap and trim; B, drip cap blocked out to extend beyond new siding and added trim.

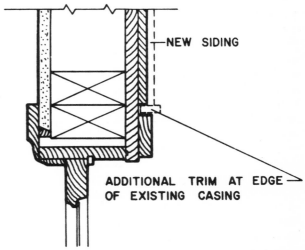

M-142 167

Figure 52.—Top view of window casing extended for new siding by adding trim at the edge of existing casing.

Another method of extending the casing would be to add a trim member to the edge of the existing casing, perpendicular to the casing (fig. 52). A wider drip cap will also be required. Exterior door trim can be extended by the same technique used for the window trim.

Any of the conventional siding materials can be used for rehabilitation, but some may be better suited to this application than others. Panel-type siding is probably one of the simplest to install and one of the most versatile. It can be applied over most surfaces, and will help to smooth out unevenness in the existing walls.

Panel Siding

Panel-type siding is available in plywood, hardboard, and particleboard, as well as numerous nonwood materials. The most popular of these are probably plywood and hardboard. Always specify exterior type for both, and the hardboard must be tempered. The grade of plywood depends on the quality of finished surface desired.

Plywood panel siding is available in a variety of textures and patterns. Sheets are 4 feet wide and are often available in lengths of 8, 9, and 10 feet. Rough-textured plywood is particularly suited to finishing with water-repellent preservative stains. Smooth-surfaced plywood can be stained, but it will not absorb as much stain as rough-textured plywood, and, therefore, the finish will not be as long lasting. Paper-overlaid plywood is particularly good for a paint finish. The paper overlay not only provides a very smooth surface, but also minimizes expansion and contraction due to moisture changes. Most textures can be purchased with vertical grooves. The most popular spacings of grooves are 2, 4, and 8 inches. Battens are often used with plain panels. They are nailed over each joint between panels and can be nailed over each stud to produce a board-and-batten effect.

In new construction, plywood applied directly over framing should be at least $^3/_8$ inch thick for 16-inch stud spacing and $^1/_2$ inch thick for 24-inch stud spacing. Grooved plywood is normally $^5/_8$ inch thick with $^3/_8$- by $^1/_4$-inch-deep grooves.

For installation over existing siding or sheathing, thinner plywood can be used; however, most of the available sidings will be in thicknesses listed above. Nail the plywood around the perimeter and at each intermediate stud, using galvanized or other rust-resistant nails spaced 7 to 8 inches apart. Use longer nails than used for applying siding directly to studs.

Some plywood siding has shiplap joints. These should be treated with a water-repellent preservative and the siding nailed at each side (fig. 53A) of the joint. Square-edge butt joints between plywood panels should be calked with a sealant (fig. 53B) with the plywood nailed at each side of the joint. Where battens are used over the joint and at intermediate studs, nail them with eightpenny galvanized nails spaced 12 inches apart. Longer nails may be required where thick existing siding or sheathing must be penetrated. Nominal 1- by 2-inch battens are commonly used.

If existing siding on gable ends is flush with the siding below the gable, some adjustment will be required in appplying panel siding in order to have a new siding at the gable extend over siding below. This is accomplished by using furring strips on the gable (fig. 54). Furring must be the same thickness as the new siding applied below. Nail a furring strip over siding or sheathing to each stud and apply the siding over the furring strips in the same manner as applying it directly to studs.

Plywood siding can be purchased with factory-applied coatings which are relatively maintenance-free. While ini-

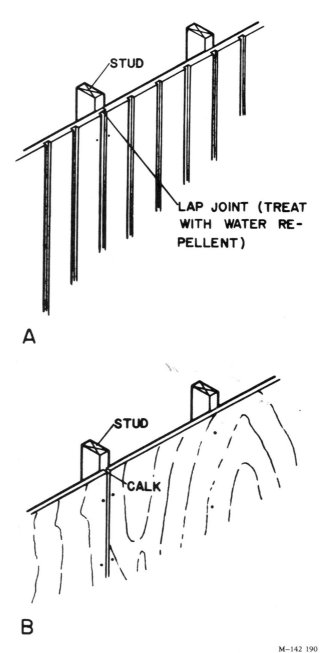

A

B

M—142 190

Figure 53.—Joint of plywood panel siding: A, shiplap joint; B, square-edge joint.

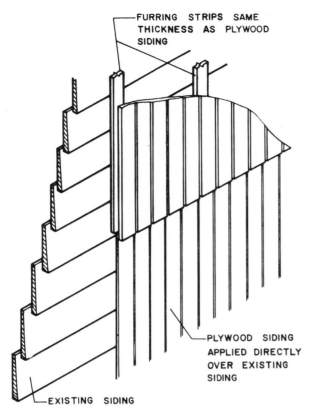

Figure 54.—Application of plywood siding at gable end.

tial cost of these products is higher than uncoated plywood, savings in maintenance may compensate for this. Such coated siding is usually applied with special nails or other connectors in accordance with fabricator's instructions.

Hardboard siding is also available in panels 4 feet wide and up to 16 feet long. It is usually $1/4$ inch thick, but may be thicker when grooved. Hardboard is usually factory-primed, and finished coats of paint are applied after installation. It is applied in the same manner as plywood.

Corners are finished by butting the panel siding against corner boards as shown for horizontal sidings (figs. 55 and 56). Use a $1^1/8$– by $1^1/8$–inch corner board at interior corners and $1^1/8$–inch by $1^1/2$– and $2^1/2$–inch boards at outside corners. Apply calking wherever siding butts against corner boards, window or door casings, and trim boards at gable ends.

Horizontal Wood Siding

Bevel siding has been one of the most popular sidings for many years. It is available in 4– to 12–inch widths. The sawn face is exposed where a rough texture is desired and a stain finish is planned. The smooth face can be exposed for either paint or stain. Siding boards should have a minimum of 1 inch horizontal lap. In application, the exposed face should be adjusted so that the butt edges coincide with the bottom of the sill and the top of the drip cap of window frames (fig. 57).

Horizontal siding must be applied over a smooth surface. If the old siding is left on, it should either be covered with panel sheathing or have furring strips nailed over each stud. Nail siding at each stud with a galvanized siding nail or other corrosion-resistant nail. Use sixpenny nails for siding less than $1/2$ inch thick and eightpenny nails for thicker siding. Locate the nail to clear the top edge of the siding course below. Butt joints should be made over a stud. Interior corners are finished by butting the siding against a corner board $1^1/8$ inches square or larger depending on thickness of siding (fig. 55). Exterior corners can be mitered, butted against corner boards $1^1/8$ inches or thicker and $1^1/2$ and $2^1/2$ inches wide (fig. 56), or covered with metal corners.

Strips of plywood or hardboard can be applied horizontally. In this application, the strips are lapped just as bevel siding but a starting strip is required at the base and a shingle wedge is required at each vertical joint (fig. 58). The starting strip should be the same thickness as the siding. Nail the siding at each vertical joint in the same manner as bevel siding. Some fabricators supply special

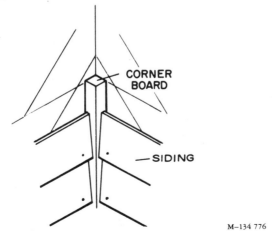

Figure 55.—Corner board for application of horizontal siding at interior corner.

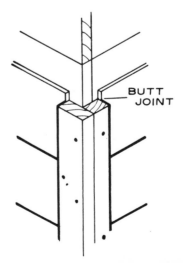

Figure 56.—Corner boards for application of horizontal siding at exterior corner.

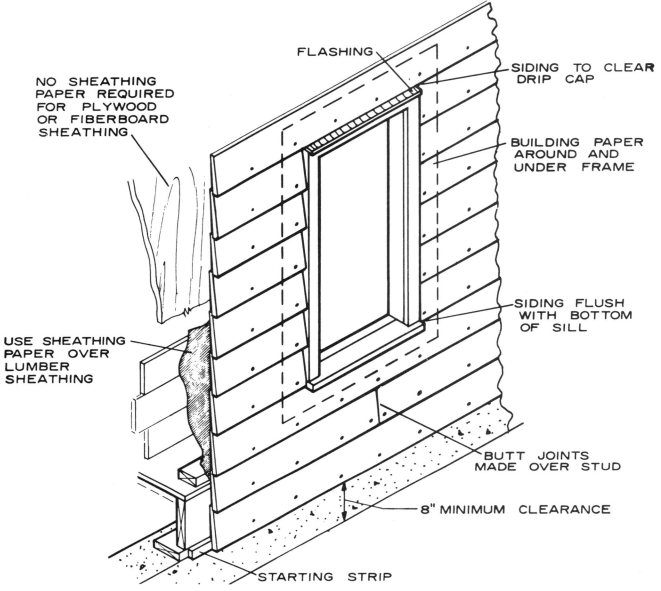

FLASHING

SIDING TO CLEAR
DRIP CAP

NO SHEATHING
PAPER REQUIRED
FOR PLYWOOD
OR FIBERBOARD
SHEATHING

BUILDING PAPER
AROUND AND
UNDER FRAME

USE SHEATHING
PAPER OVER
LUMBER
SHEATHING

SIDING FLUSH
WITH BOTTOM
OF SILL

BUTT JOINTS
MADE OVER STUD

8" MINIMUM CLEARANCE

STARTING STRIP

M–134 712

Figure 57.—Application of bevel siding to coincide with window sill and drip cap.

clips for applying the siding. When these are used, follow the fabricator's instructions.

Vertical Wood Siding

Vertical siding is available in a variety of patterns. Probably the most popular is matched (tongued-and-grooved) boards. Vertical siding can be nailed to 1–inch sheathing boards or to $5/8$– and $3/4$–inch plywood. Furring strips must be used over thinner plywood because the plywood itself will not have sufficient nail-holding capacity. When the existing sheathing is thinner than $5/8$ inch, apply 1– by 4–inch nailers horizontally, spaced 16 to 24 inches apart vertically. Then nail the vertical siding to the nailers. Blind-nail through the tongue at each nailer with galvanized sevenpenny finish nails. When boards are nomi-

nal 6 inches or wider, also face-nail at midwidth with an eightpenny galvanized nail (fig. 59). Vertical siding can be applied over existing siding by nailing through the siding into the sheathing.

Another popular vertical siding is comprised of various combinations of boards and battens. It also must be nailed to a thick sheathing or to horizontal nailers. The first board or batten should be nailed with one galvanized eightpenny nail at center or, for wide boards, two nails spaced 1 inch each side of center. Close spacing is important to prevent splitting if the boards shrink. The top board or batten is then nailed with twelvepenny nails, being careful to miss the underboard and nail only through the space between adjacent boards (fig. 60). Use only corrosion-resistant nails. Galvanized nails are not recommended for some materials, so be sure to follow siding manufacturer's instructions.

38

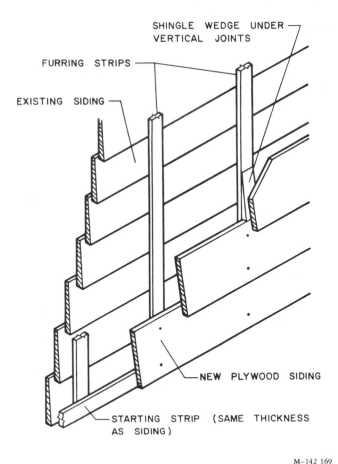

SHINGLE WEDGE UNDER
VERTICAL JOINTS

FURRING STRIPS

EXISTING SIDING

NEW PLYWOOD SIDING

STARTING STRIP (SAME THICKNESS
AS SIDING)

M–142 169

Figure 58.—Application of plywood as lap siding.

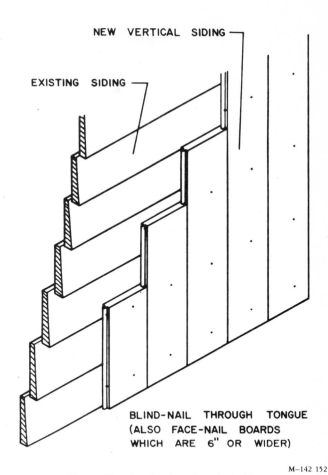

NEW VERTICAL SIDING

EXISTING SIDING

BLIND-NAIL THROUGH TONGUE
(ALSO FACE-NAIL BOARDS
WHICH ARE 6" OR WIDER)

M–142 152

Figure 59.—Application of vertical siding.

Wood Shingle and Shake Siding

Some architectural styles may be well suited to the use of shakes or shingles for siding. They give a rustic appearance and can be left unfinished, if desired, to weather naturally. They may be applied in single or double courses over wood or plywood sheathing. Where shingles are applied over existing siding which is uneven or over a nonwood sheathing, use 1– by 3– or 1– by 4–inch wood nailing strips applied horizontally as a base for the shingles. Spacing of the nailing strips will depend on the length and exposure of the shingles. Apply the shingles with about $1/8$– to $1/4$– inch space between adjacent shingles to allow for expansion during rainy weather.

The single-course method consists of simply laying one course over the other similar to lap siding application. Second-grade shingles can be used because only one-half or less of the butt portion is exposed (fig. 61).

The double-course method of laying shingles consists of applying an undercourse and nailing a top course directly over it with a $1/4$– to $1/2$–inch projection of the butt over the lower course shingle (fig. 62). With this system, less lap is used between courses. The undercourse shingles can be lower quality, such as third grade or the undercourse grade. The top course should be first grade because of the shingle length exposed.

BOARD

BOARD AND BATTEN

SINGLE
NAILING

BATTEN

FIRST
NAIL

BATTEN AND BOARD

SPACE 16" VERTICALLY
WHEN WOOD
SHEATHING IS USED

DOUBLE NAILING

BOARD AND BOARD

M–134 621

Figure 60.—Application of vertical wood siding.

Recommended exposure distances for shingles and shakes are given in table 3.

Regardless of the method of applying the shingles, all joints must be broken so that the vertical butt joints of the upper shingles are at least 1 1/2 inches from the undershingle joint.

Use rust-resistant nails for all shingle applications. Shingles up to 8 inches wide should be nailed with two nails. Wider shingles should be secured with three nails. Threepenny or fourpenny zinc-coated "shingle" nails are commonly used in single-coursing. Zinc-coated nails with small flat heads are commonly used for double-coursing where nails are exposed. Use fivepenny for the top course and threepenny or fourpenny for the undercourse. When plywood sheathing less than 3/4 inch thick is used, threaded nails are required to obtain sufficient holding power. Nails

Table 3.—*Exposure distances for wood shingles and shakes on sidewalls*

Material	Length	Maximum exposure		
		Single coursing	Double coursing	
			No. 1 grade	No. 2 grade
	In.	*In.*	*In.*	*In.*
Shingles	16	7 1/2	12	10
	18	8 1/2	14	11
	24	11 1/2	16	14
Shakes (handsplit and re-sawn)	18	8 1/2	14	—
	24	11 1/2	20	—
	32	15	—	—

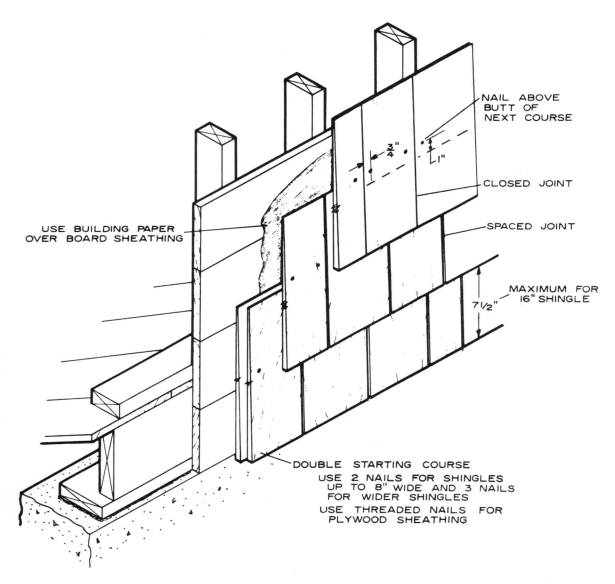

NAIL ABOVE BUTT OF NEXT COURSE

CLOSED JOINT

SPACED JOINT

MAXIMUM FOR 16" SHINGLE

3/4"

1"

7 1/2"

USE BUILDING PAPER OVER BOARD SHEATHING

DOUBLE STARTING COURSE
USE 2 NAILS FOR SHINGLES UP TO 8" WIDE AND 3 NAILS FOR WIDER SHINGLES
USE THREADED NAILS FOR PLYWOOD SHEATHING

M-134 610

Figure 61.—Single-course application of shingle siding.

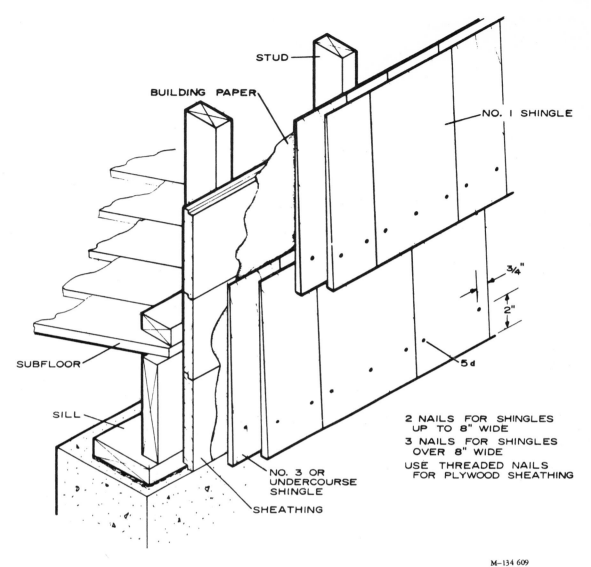

STUD

BUILDING PAPER

NO. I SHINGLE

3/4"

2"

5 d

2 NAILS FOR SHINGLES
UP TO 8" WIDE
3 NAILS FOR SHINGLES
OVER 8" WIDE
USE THREADED NAILS
FOR PLYWOOD SHEATHING

NO. 3 OR
UNDERCOURSE
SHINGLE

SHEATHING

SUBFLOOR

SILL

M–134 609

Figure 62.—Double-course application of shingle siding.

should be $3/4$ inch from the edge. They should be 1 inch above the horizontal butt line of the next higher course in the single-course application and 2 inches above the bottom of the shingle or shake in the double-course application.

Masonry Veneer

Where brick or stone veneer is used as siding, mortar may become loose and crumble, or uneven settlement may cause cracks. In either case, new mortar should be applied both to keep out moisture and to improve appearance. Repair is accomplished in much the same manner as for masonry foundations, except that more attention to appearance is required. After removing all loose mortar and brushing the joint to remove dust and loose particles, dampen the surface. Then apply mortar and tamp it well into the joint for a good bond. Pointing of joints should conform to existing joints. Particular care should be exercised in keeping mortar off the face of the brick or stone unless the veneer is to be painted.

Many older houses used soft bricks and porous stone trim. After repair of the cracks and mortar joints, the entire surface may require treatment with transparent waterproofing. Painted, stained, or dirty brick and stone can be restored to its original appearance by sandblasting. It can then be repainted or waterproofed. Caution should be used in sandblasting soft stone and brick.

ROOF SYSTEM

The first steps in repairing a roof system are to level sagging ridge poles and straighten sagging rafters. Then the new roof covering can be applied to a smooth, flat surface.

Framing

The sagging ridgepole can sometimes be leveled by jacking it at points between supports and installing props to hold it in a level position. When this is done, the jack

41

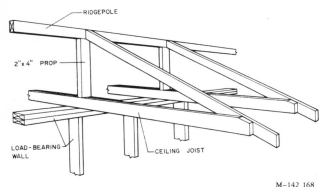

RIDGEPOLE

2"x4" PROP

LOAD-BEARING
WALL

CEILING JOIST

M-142 168

Figure 63.—Prop to hold sagging ridgepole in level position.

must be located where the load can be traced down through the structure so the ultimate bearing is directly on the foundation. Where there is no conveniently located bearing partition, install a beam under the ridge and transfer load to bearing points. After the ridgepole is jacked to a level position, cut a 2 by 4 just long enough to fit between the ceiling joist and ridgepole or beam and nail it at both ends (fig. 63). For a short ridgepole, one prop may be sufficient. Additional props should be added as needed. In some repairs the addition of collar beams may be sufficient without requiring props. Where rafters are sagging, nail a new rafter to the side of the old one after forcing the new rafter ends into their proper position. Permanent set in the old rafters cannot be removed.

Sheathing

Sheathing may have sagged between rafters, resulting in a wavy roof surface. Where this condition exists, new sheathing is required. Often the sheathing can be nailed right over the old roofing. This saves the labor of removing old roofing and a big cleanup job. Wood shingles which show any indication of decay should be completely removed before new sheathing is applied. Where wood shingles are excessively cupped or otherwise warped, they should also be removed. Wood shingle and slate roofs of older houses were often installed on furring strips rather than on solid sheathing.

Sheathing nailed over existing sheathing or over sheathing and roofing must be secured with longer nails than would normally be used. Nails should penetrate the framing $1\frac{1}{4}$ to $1\frac{1}{2}$ inches. Nail edges of plywood sheathing at 6–inch spacing and to intermediate framing members at 12–inch spacing. Apply the plywood with the length perpendicular to the rafters. For built-up roofs, if the plywood does not have tongued-and-grooved edges, use clips at unsupported edges. Clips are commercially available and should be installed in accordance with fabricator's instructions. For 16-inch rafter spacing, $\frac{3}{8}$-inch plywood is the minimum thickness to be used and $\frac{1}{2}$-inch-thick plywood is preferable.

Adding Roof Overhang

The addition of a roof overhang, where there is none, will soon pay for itself in reduced maintenance on siding

and exterior trim. Without the overhang, water washes down the face of the wall, creating moisture problems in the siding and trim and, consequently, more frequent painting is required. Additional roof overhang also does much to improve the appearance of the house.

Where new sheathing is being added, the sheathing can be extended beyond the edge of the existing roof to provide some overhang. This is a minimum solution and the extension should not be more than 12 inches where $\frac{1}{2}$-inch plywood sheathing is used. Any greater extension would require some type of framing. Framing can usually be extended at the eave by adding to each rafter. First, remove the frieze board, or, in the case of a closed cornice, remove the facia. Nail a 2 by 4 to the side of each rafter, letting it extend beyond the wall the amount of the desired overhang. The 2 by 4 should extend inside the wall a distance equal to the overhang (fig. 64A). Framing for an overhang at the gable ends can be accomplished by adding a box frame. Extensions of the ridge beam and eave facia are required to support this boxed framing. An alternate extension is possible with plank placed flat, cut into gable framing, and extending back to the first rafter (fig. 64B).

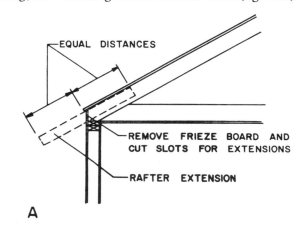

EQUAL DISTANCES

REMOVE FRIEZE BOARD AND
CUT SLOTS FOR EXTENSIONS

RAFTER EXTENSION

A

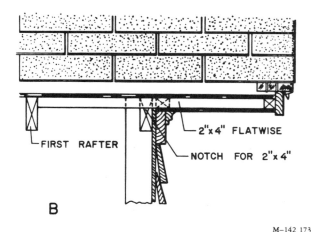

FIRST RAFTER

2"x4" FLATWISE

NOTCH FOR 2"x4"

B

M-142 173

Figure 64.—Extension of roof overhang: A, rafter extension at eaves; B, extension at gable end.

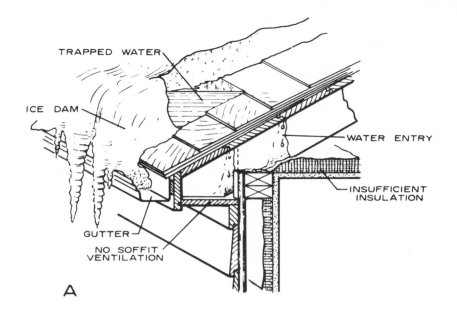

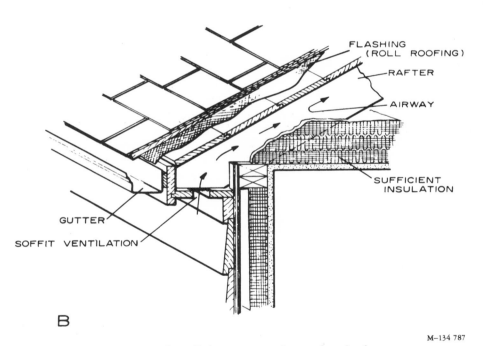

M-134 787

Figure 65.—Flashing and ventilation to prevent damage from ice dams.

Roof Coverings

A wide variety of roof coverings is available, and most can be used in rehabilitation in the same manner as for new construction. Sometimes there are local code requirements for fire safety. First cost usually influences the choice. In most houses the roof is a major design element and the covering material must fit the house design. Heavy materials such as tile or slate should not be used unless they replace the same material or unless the roof framing is strengthened to support the additional load. The most popular covering materials for pitched roofs are wood, asphalt, and asbestos shingles. These can be applied directly over old shingles or over sheathing as previously described; however, if two layers of shingles exist from previous reroofing, it may be well to remove the old roofing before proceeding. Roll roofing is sometimes used for particularly low-cost applications or over porches with relatively low-pitched roofs. The most common covering for flat or low-pitched roofs is built-up roof with a gravel topping.

An underlay of 15— or 30—pound asphalt-saturated felt should be used in moderate and lower slope roofs covered

43

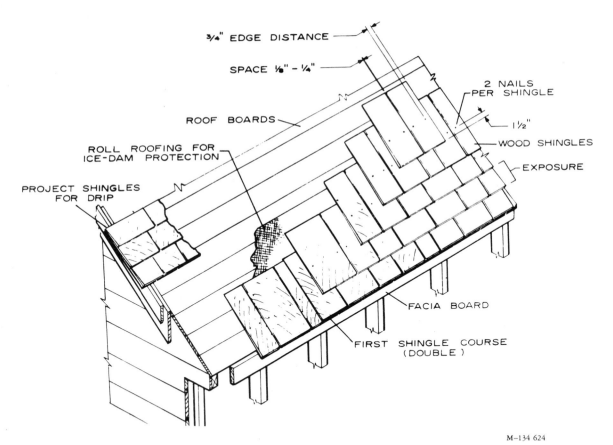

Figure 66.—Application of wood-shingle roofing over boards.

M–134 624

with asphalt, asbestos, or slate shingles, or tile roofing. It is not commonly used under wood shingles or shakes. A 45–pound or heavier smooth-surface roll roofing should be used as a flashing along the eave line in areas where moderate to severe snowfalls occur. The flashing should extend to a point 36 inches inside the warm wall. If two strips are required, use mastic to seal the joint. Also use mastic to seal end joints. This flashing gives protection from ice dams (fig. 65). Ice dams are formed when melting snow runs down the roof and freezes at the colder cornice area. The ice gradually forms a dam that backs up water under the shingles. The wide flashing at the eave will minimize the chances of this water entering the ceiling or the wall. Good attic ventilation and sufficient ceiling insulation are also important in eliminating ice dams. This will be described in the section entitled "Ventilation." Roll roofing 36 inches wide is also required at all valleys.

Where shingle application is over old wood or asphalt shingles, industry recommendations include certain preparations. First remove about 6–inch–wide strips of old shingles along the eaves and gables, and apply nominal 1–inch boards at these locations. Thinner boards may be necessary where application is over old asphalt shingles. Remove the old covering from ridges or hips and replace the bevel siding with butt edges up. Place a strip of lumber over each valley to separate old metal flashing from new. Double the first shingle course.

Wood shingles.—Wood shingles used for house roofs should be No. 1 grade which are all heartwood, all edge

grain, and tapered. Principal species used commercially are western redcedar and redwood, which have heartwood with high decay resistance and low shrinkage. Widths of shingles vary, and the narrower shingles are most often found in the lower grades. Recommended exposures for common shingle sizes are shown in table 4.

General rules to follow in applying wood shingles are (fig. 66):

1. Extend shingles $1^1/_2$ to 2 inches beyond the eave line and about $^3/_4$ inch beyond the rake (gable) edge.

2. Nail each shingle with two rust-resistant nails spaced about $^3/_4$ inch from the edge and $1^1/_2$ inches above the butt line of the next course. Use threepenny nails for 16– and 18–inch shingles and fourpenny nails for 24–inch shingles. Where shingles are applied over old wood shingles, use longer nails to penetrate through the old roofing and into the sheathing. A ring-shank nail (threaded) is recommended where the plywood roof sheathing is less than $^1/_2$ inch thick.

3. Allow a $^1/_8$– to $^1/_4$–inch space between each shingle for expansion when wet. Lap vertical joints at least $1^1/_2$ inches by the shingles in the course above. Space the joints in succeeding courses so that the joint in one course is not in line with the joint in the second course above it.

4. Shingle away from valleys, selecting and precutting wide valley shingles. The valley should be 4 inches wide at the top and increase in width at the rate of $^1/_8$ inch per foot from the top. Use valley flashing with a standing seam. Do not nail through the metal. Valley flashing should be a

44

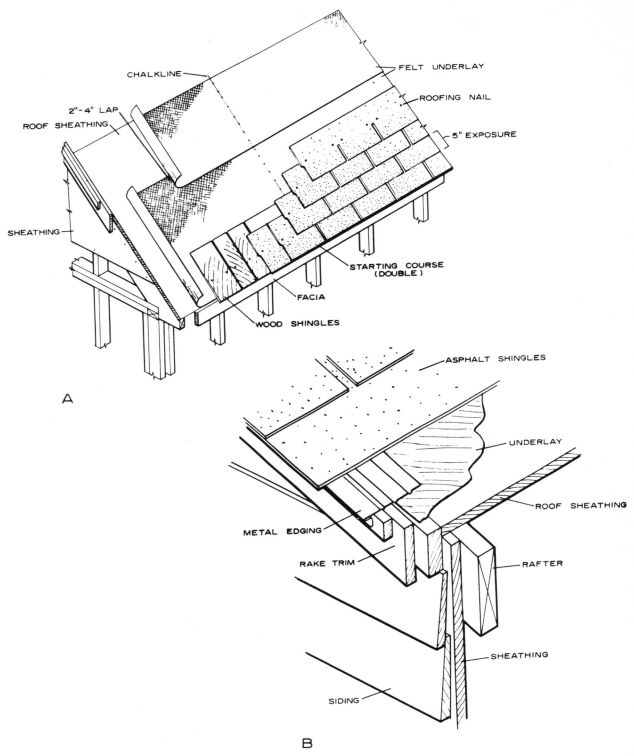

CHALKLINE

FELT UNDERLAY

ROOFING NAIL

2"-4" LAP

ROOF SHEATHING

5" EXPOSURE

SHEATHING

STARTING COURSE
(DOUBLE)

FACIA

WOOD SHINGLES

A

ASPHALT SHINGLES

UNDERLAY

ROOF SHEATHING

METAL EDGING

RAKE TRIM

RAFTER

SHEATHING

SIDING

B

M–142 198

Figure 67.—Application of asphalt-shingle roofing over plywood: A, with strip shingles; B, metal edging at gable end.

minimum of 24 inches wide for roof slopes under 4 in 12; 18 inches wide for roof slopes of 4 in 12 to 7 in 12; and 12 inches wide for roof slopes of 7 in 12 and over.

5. Place a metal edging along the gable end of roof to aid in guiding the water away from the endwalls.

Wood shakes.—Apply wood shakes in much the same manner as shingles, except longer nails must be used because the shakes are thicker. Shakes have a greater exposure than shingles because of their length. Exposure distances are 8 inches for 18–inch shakes, 10 inches for 24–

45

Table 4.—*Recommended exposure for wood shingles*

Shingle length	Shingle thickness (green)	Maximum exposure	
		Slope less[1] than 4 in 12	Slope 4 in 12 and over
In.		*In.*	*In.*
16	5 butts in 2 in.	3¾	5
18	5 butts in 2¼ in.	4¼	5½
24	4 butts in 2 in.	5¾	7½

[1] Minimum slope for main roofs—4 in 12. Minimum slope for porch roofs—3 in 12.

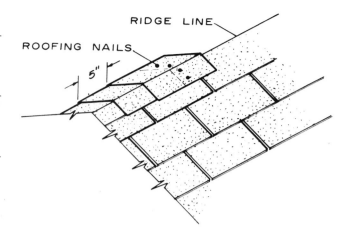

RIDGE LINE
ROOFING NAILS
5"

M–135 151

Figure 68.—Boston ridge using asphalt shingles.

inch shakes, and 13 inches for 32–inch shakes. Butts are often laid unevenly to create a rustic appearance. An 18–inch–wide underlay of 30–pound asphalt felt should be used between each course to prevent wind-driven snow from entering between the rough faces of the shakes. Position the underlay above the butt edge of the shakes a distance equal to double the weather exposure. Where exposure distance is less than one-third the total length, underlay is not usually required.

Asphalt shingles.—The most common type of asphalt shingle is the square-butt strip shingle, which is 12 by 36 inches, has three tabs, and is usually laid with 5 inches exposed to the weather. Bundles should be piled flat so that strips will not curl when the bundles are opened for use. An underlayment of 15–pound saturated felt is often used. Table 5 shows the requirements in applying underlayment.

Begin application of the roofing by first applying a wood-shingle course or a metal edging along the eave line (fig. 67A). The first course of asphalt shingles is doubled and extended downward beyond the wood shingles (or edging) about ½ inch to prevent the water from backing up under the shingles. A ½–inch projection should also be used at the rake (fig. 67B). Make several chalklines on the underlayment parallel to the roof slope to serve as guides in alining the shingles so that tabs are in a straight line. Use manufacturer's directions in securing the shingles. Nailing each 12– by 36–inch strip with six 1–inch galvanized roofing nails (fig. 67), is good practice in areas of high winds. Seal-tab or lock shingles should be used in these areas. When a nail penetrates a crack or knothole, remove the nail, seal the hole, and replace the nail in sound wood.

If the nail is not in sound wood, it will gradually work out and cause a hump in the shingle above it.

Built-up roof.—Built-up roof coverings are limited to flat or low-pitched roofs and are installed by contractors that specialize in this work. The roof consists of three, four, or five layers of roofers' felt, with each layer mopped down with tar or asphalt. The final surface is then coated with asphalt and usually covered with gravel embedded in asphalt or tar.

Other roof coverings.—Other roof coverings, such as asbestos, slate, tile, and metal, require specialized applicators, so their application is not described in detail. They are generally more expensive and are much less widely used than wood or asphalt shingles and built-up roofs.

Ridge

The Boston ridge is the most common method of treating the roof ridge and is also applicable to hips. Where asphalt shingles are used, cut the 12– by 36–inch strips into 12– by 12–inch sections. Bend them slightly and use in a lap fashion over the ridge with a 5–inch exposure distance (fig. 68). Locate nails where they will be covered by the lap of the next section. A small spot of asphalt cement under each exposed edge will give a positive seal.

Wood-shingle roofs can also be finished with a Boston ridge. Flashing should first be placed over the ridge. Six–inch–wide shingles are alternately lapped, fitted, and

Table 5.—*Underlayment requirements for asphalt shingles*

Underlayment[1]	Minimum roof slope	
	Double coverage[2] shingles	Triple coverage[2] shingles
Not required	7 in 12	[3]4 in 12
Single	[3]4 in 12	[4]3 in 12
Double	2 in 12	2 in 12

[1] Headlap for single coverage of underlayment should be 2 in. and for double coverage 19 in.
[2] Double coverage for a 12– by 36–in. shingle is usually an exposure of about 5 in. and about 4 in. for triple coverage.
[3] May be 3 in 12 for porch roofs.
[4] May be 2 in 12 for porch roofs.

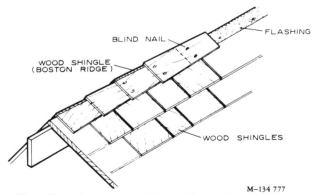

FLASHING
BLIND NAIL
WOOD SHINGLE (BOSTON RIDGE)
WOOD SHINGLES

M–134 777

Figure 69.—Boston ridge using wood shingles.

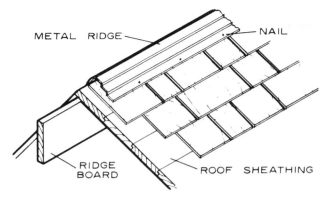

Figure 70.—Metal ridge roll.

M–134 777

blind-nailed (fig. 69). Exposed shingle edges are alternately lapped.

A metal ridge roll can also be used on asphalt-shingle or wood-shingle roofs (fig. 70). This ridge of copper, galvanized iron, or aluminum is formed to the roof slope.

OPENINGS

WINDOWS

Windows may need repair, replacement, or relocation. Until recent years, windows were not generally treated with a preservative, so moisture may have gotten into some joints and resulted in decay. Also, older windows may allow more air infiltration than newer types. It will often be desirable to replace the windows. This is not difficult where the same size window can be used; however, where the window size is no longer produced, replacement of the window will also mean reframing it.

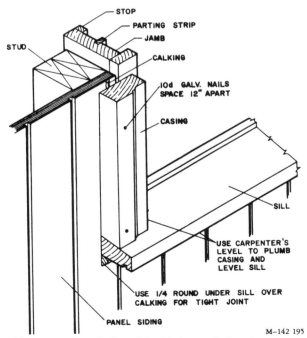

Figure 71.—Installation of double-hung window frame.

M–142 195

The sequence of window replacement will depend on the type of siding used. Where new panel siding is being applied, the window is installed after the siding. Where horizontal siding is used, the window must be installed before the siding.

Repair of Existing Windows

Where the wood in windows is showing some signs of deterioration but the window is still in good operating condition, a water-repellent preservative may arrest further decay. First, remove existing paint; then brush on the preservative, let it dry, and repaint the window. Paint cannot be used over some preservatives, so make sure a paintable preservative is used.

Double-hung sash may bind against the stops, jambs, or the parting strip. Before doing any repair, try waxing the parts in contact. If this doesn't eliminate the problem, try to determine where the sash is binding. Excessive paint buildup is a common cause of sticking and can be corrected by removing paint from stops and parting strips. Nailed stops (fig. 71) can be moved away from the sash slightly; if stops are fastened by screws, it will probably be easier to remove the stop and plane it lightly on the face contacting the sash. Loosening the contact between sash and stop too much will result in excessive air infiltration at the window. If the sash is binding against the jamb, remove the sash and plane the vertical edges slightly.

It may be desirable to add full-width weatherstrip and spring balance units to provide a good airtight window that will not bind. These are easily installed, requiring only removal of parting strip and stops. Install the units in accordance with manufacturer's instructions and replace the stops.

Replacement of Existing Windows

If windows require extensive repairs, it will probably be more economical to replace them. New windows are usually purchased as a complete unit, including sash, frame, and exterior trim. These are easily installed where a window of the same size and type is removed. Many older houses have tall, narrow windows of sizes that are no longer commercially produced, and in some cases it may be desirable to change size or type of window. Most window manufacturers list rough-opening sizes for each of their windows. Some general rules to follow for rough-opening size are:

A. *Double-hung window (single unit)*
Rough opening width = glass width *plus* 6 inches
Rough opening height = total glass height *plus* 10 inches
B. *Casement window (two sash)*
Rough opening width = total glass width *plus* $11^1/4$ inches
Rough opening height = total glass height *plus* $6^3/8$ inches

After the existing window is removed, take off the interior wall covering to the rough opening width for the new window. If a larger window must be centered in the

47

same location as the old one, half the necessary additional width must be cut from each side; otherwise, the entire additional width may be cut from one side. For windows 3½ feet or less in width, no temporary support of ceiling and roof should be required. Where windows more than 3½ feet wide are to be installed, provide some temporary support for the ceiling and roof before removing existing framing in bearing walls. Remove framing to the width of the new window and frame the window as shown in figure 72. The header must be supported at both ends by cripple studs. Headers are made up of two 2–inch–thick members, usually spaced with lath or wood strips to produce the same width as the 2 by 4 stud space. The following sizes might be used as a guide for headers:

Maximum span	Header size
Ft	*In.*
3½	Two 2 by 6
5	Two 2 by 8
6½	Two 2 by 10
8	Two 2 by 12

For wider openings, independent design may be necessary. Do not oversize headers on the theory that, if a little is good, more is better. Cross-grain shrinkage causes distortion, and should be kept to a minimum.

Cut the sheathing, or panel siding used without sheathing, to the size of the rough opening. If bevel siding is used, it must be cut to the size of the window trim so that it will butt against the window casing (fig. 57). Determine the place to cut the siding by inserting the preassembled window frame in the rough opening and marking the siding around the outside edge of the casing.

Before installing the window frame in the rough opening, precautions must be taken to insure that water and wind do not come in around the finished window. Where panel siding is used, place a ribbon of calking sealant (rubber or similar base) over the siding at the location of the side and head casing (fig. 73). Where horizontal siding is used over sheathing, loosen the siding around the opening and slide strips of 15–pound asphalt felt between the sheathing and siding around the opening (fig. 57).

Place the frame in the rough opening, preferably with the sash in place to keep it square, and level the sill with a carpenter's level. Use shims under the sill on the inside if necessary. Check the side casing and jamb for level and square; then nail the frame in place with tenpenny galvanized nails. Nail through the casing into the side studs and header (fig. 71), spacing the nails about 12 inches apart. When double-hung windows are used, slide the sash up and down while nailing the frame to be sure that the sash works freely. For installation over panel siding, place a ribbon of calking sealer at the junction of the siding and the sill and install a small molding, such as a quarter-round, over the calking.

Relocation of Windows

It may be desirable to move a window to a different location or to eliminate a window and add a new one at

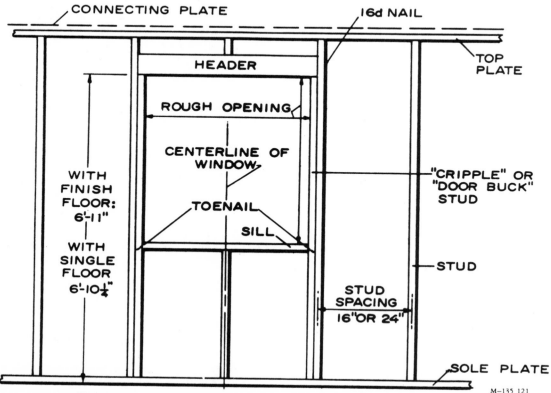

Figure 72.—Framing at window opening and height of window and door headers.

M–135 121

48

another location. The method for installing a window is described in the preceding section. Where a window is removed, close the opening as follows: Add 2 by 4 vertical framing members spaced no more than 16 inches apart. Keep framing in line with existing studs under the window or in sequence with wall studs so covering materials can be nailed to them easily. Toenail new framing to the old window header and to the sill using three eightpenny or tenpenny nails at each joint. Install sheathing of the same thickness as that existing, add insulation, and apply a vapor barrier on the inside face of the framing. Make sure the vapor barrier covers the rough framing of the existing window and overlaps any vapor barrier in the remainder of the wall. Insulation and vapor barriers are discussed more fully in separate sections. Apply interior and exterior wall covering to match the existing coverings on the house.

Storm Windows

In cold climates, storm windows are necessary for comfort, for economy of heating, and to avoid damage from excessive condensation on the inside face of the window. If old windows are not standard sizes, storm windows must be made by building a frame to fit the existing window and fitting glass to the frame. Storm windows are commercially available to fit all standard size windows. One of the most practical types is the self-storing or combination storm and screen. These have minor adjustments for width and height, and can be custom fabricated for odd-size windows at a moderate cost.

DOORS

Doors in houses of all ages frequently cause problems by sticking and by failure to latch. To remedy the sticking door, first determine where it is sticking. If the frame is not critically out of square some minor adjustments may remedy the situation. The top of the door could be planed without removing the door. If the side of the door is sticking near the top or bottom, the excess width can also be planed off without removing the door; however, the edge will have to be refinished or repainted. If the side of the door sticks near the latch or over the entire height of the door, remove the hinges and plane the hinge edge. Then additional routing is required before the hinges are replaced. Where the door is binding on the hinge edge, the hinges may be routed too deeply. This can be corrected by loosening the hinge leaf and adding a filler under it to bring it out slightly. If the latch does not close, remove the strike plate and shim it out slightly. Replace the strike plate by first placing a filler, such as a matchstick, in the screw hole and reinserting the screw so that the strike plate is relocated slightly away from the stop.

Exterior Doors

If exterior doors are badly weathered, it may be desirable to replace them rather than attempt a repair. Doors can be purchased separately or with frames, including exterior side and head casing with rabbeted jamb and a sill (fig. 74).

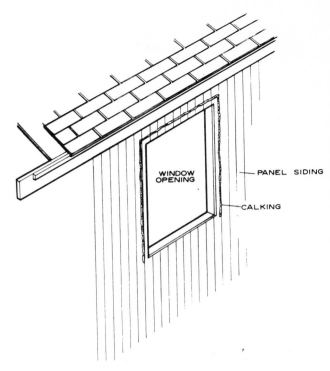

M–135 162

Figure 73.—Calking around window opening before installing frame.

Exterior doors should be either panel or solid-core flush type. Several styles are available, most of them featuring some type of glazing (fig. 75). Hollow-core flush doors should be limited to interior use, except in warm climates, because they warp excessively during the heating season when used as exterior doors. Standard height for exterior doors is 6 feet 8 inches. Standard thickness is $1^3/4$ inches. The main door should be 3 feet wide, and the service or rear door should be at least 2 feet 6 inches and preferably up to 3 feet wide.

Where rough framing is required either for a new door location or because old framing is not square, provide header and cripple studs as shown in figure 72. Rough opening height should be the height of the door plus $2^1/4$ inches above the finished floor; width should be the width of the door plus $2^1/2$ inches. Use doubled 2 by 6's for headers and fasten them in place with two sixteenpenny nails through the stud into each member. If the stud space on each side of the door is not accessible, toenail the header to studs. Nail cripple (door buck) studs, supporting the header, on each side of the opening to the full stud with twelvepenny nails spaced about 16 inches apart and staggered.

After sheathing or panel siding is placed over the framing, leaving only the rough opening, the door frame can be installed. Apply a ribbon of calking sealer on each side and above the opening where the casing will fit right over it. Place the door frame in the opening and secure it by nailing through the side and head casing. Nail hinge side first. In a new installation the floor joists and header must be trimmed to receive the sill before the frame can be installed (fig. 76). The top of the sill should be the same height as

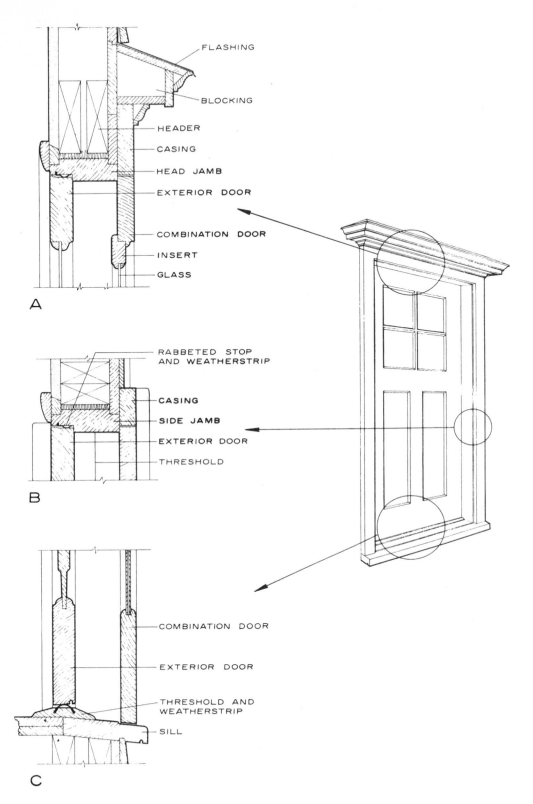

FLASHING

BLOCKING

HEADER

CASING

HEAD JAMB

EXTERIOR DOOR

COMBINATION DOOR

INSERT

GLASS

A

RABBETED STOP
AND WEATHERSTRIP

CASING

SIDE JAMB

EXTERIOR DOOR

THRESHOLD

B

COMBINATION DOOR

EXTERIOR DOOR

THRESHOLD AND
WEATHERSTRIP

SILL

C

M-134 683

Figure 74.—Exterior door and frame. Exterior door and combination-door (screen and storm) cross sections: A, head jamb; B, side jamb; C, sill.

the finish floor so that the threshold can be installed over the joint. Shim the sill when necessary so that it will have full bearing on the floor framing. When joists are parallel to the sill, headers and a short support member are necessary at the edge of the sill. Use a quarter-round molding in combination with calking under the door sill when a panel

50

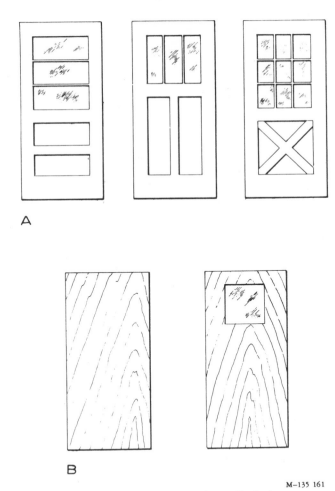

A

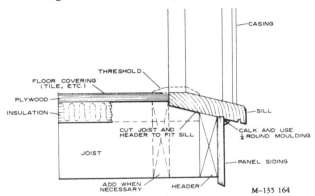

B

M-135 161

Figure 75.—Exterior doors: A, panel type, B, flush type.

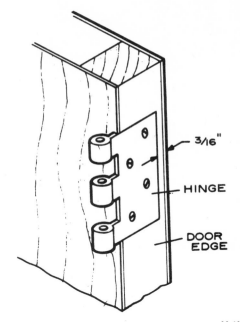

M-135 179

Figure 77.—Installation of door hinges.

toward the side that will fit against stops. Clearances are shown in figure 78. Carefully measure the opening width and plane the edge for the proper side clearances. Next, square and trim the top of the door for proper fit; then saw off the bottom for the proper floor clearance. All edges should then be sealed to minimize entrance of moisture.

In cold climates, weatherstrip all exterior doors. Check weatherstripping on old doors, and replace it where there is indication of wear. Also consider adding storm doors in cold climates. The storm door will not only save on heat,

siding or other single exterior covering is used. Install the threshold over the junction with the finish floor by nailing it to the floor and sill with finishing nails.

Exterior doors are usually purchased with an entry lock set which is easily installed. Any trimming to reduce the width of the door is done on the hinge edge. Hinges are routed or mortised into the edge of the door with about $3/16$– or $1/4$–inch back spacing (fig. 77). In-swinging exterior doors require $3^1/2$– by $3^1/2$–inch loose-pin hinges. Nonremovable pins are used on out-swinging doors. Use three hinges to minimize warping. Bevel edges slightly

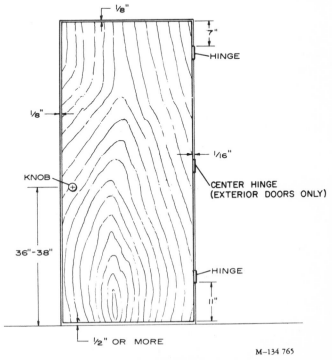

M-134 765

Figure 78.—Door clearances.

Figure 76.—Door installation at sill.

51

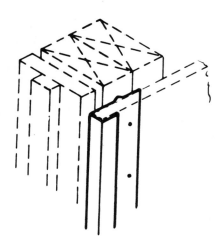

Figure 79.—Metal casing used with drywall.

but will protect the surface of the exterior door from the weather and help prevent warping.

Interior Doors

If a new interior door is added or the framing is replaced, the opening should be rough framed in a manner similar to that for exterior doors. Rough framing width is $2^1/2$ inches plus the door width; height is 2 inches plus the door height above the finished floor. The head jamb and two side jambs are the same width as the overall wall thickness where wood casing is used. Where metal casing is used with drywall (fig. 79), the jamb width is the same as the stud depth. Jambs are often purchased in precut sets, and can even be purchased complete with stops and with the door prehung in the frame. Jambs can also easily be made in a small shop with a table or radial-arm saw (fig. 80). The prehung door is by far the simplest to install, and is usually the most economical because of the labor saving. Even where the door and jambs are purchased separately, the installation is simplified by prehanging the door in the frame at the building site. The door then serves as a jig to set the frame in place quite easily. Before installing the door, temporarily put in place the narrow wood strips used as stops. Stops are usually $^7/_{16}$ inch thick and may be $1^1/2$ to $2^1/4$ inches wide. Install them with a mitered joint at the junction of the head and side jambs. A 45° bevel cut 1 to $1^1/2$ inches

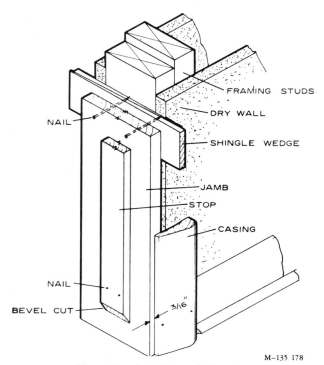

Figure 81.—Installation of door trim.

above the finish floor will eliminate a dirt pocket and make cleaning easier (fig. 81). This is called a sanitary stop.

Fit the door to the frame, using the clearances shown in figure 78. Bevel edges slightly toward side that will fit against stops. Route or mortise the hinges into the edge of the door with about a $^3/_{16}$– or $^1/_4$-inch back spacing. Make adjustments, if necessary, to provide sufficient edge distance so that screws have good penetration in the wood. For interior doors, use two 3– by 3–inch loose-pin hinges. If a router is not available, mark the hinge outline and depth of cut, and remove the wood with a wood chisel. The surface

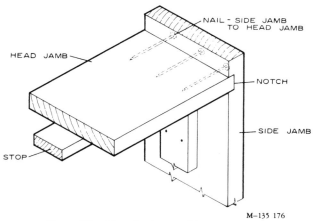

Figure 80.—Door jamb assembly.

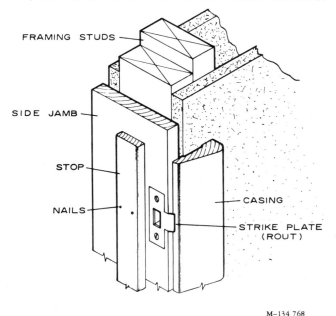

Figure 82.—Installation of door strike plate.

of the hinge should be flush with the wood surface. After attaching the hinge to the door with screws, place the door in the opening, block it for proper clearances, and mark the location of door hinges on the jamb. Remove the door and route the jamb the thickness of the hinge half. Install the hinge halves on the jamb, place the door in the opening, and insert the pins.

Lock sets are classed as: (a) Entry lock sets (decorative keyed lock), (b) privacy lock set (inside lock control with a safety slot for opening from the outside), (c) lock set (keyed lock), and (d) latch set (without lock). The lock set is usually purchased with the door and may even be installed with the door. If not installed, directions are provided, including paper templates which provide for exact location of holes. After the latch is installed, mark the location of the latch on the jamb when the door is in a near-closed position. Mark the outline of the strike plate for this position and route the jamb so the strike plate will be flush with the face of the jamb (fig. 82).

The stops which were temporarily nailed in place can now be permanently installed. Nail the stop on the lock side first, setting it against the door face when the door is latched. Nail the stops with finishing nails or brads $1^1/_2$ inches long and spaced in pairs about 16 inches apart. The stop at the hinge side of the door should allow a clearance of $^1/_{32}$ inch (fig. 83).

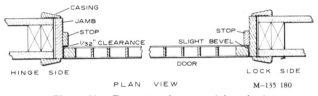

Figure 83.—Door stop clearances (plan view).

To install a new door frame, place the frame in the opening and plumb and fasten the hinge side of the frame first. Use shingle wedges between the side jamb and the rough door buck to plumb the jamb (fig. 81). Place wedge sets at hinge and latch locations plus intermediate locations along the height, and nail the jamb with pairs of eight-penny nails at each wedge area. Continue installation by fastening the opposite jamb in the same manner. After the door jambs are installed, cut off the shingle wedges flush with the wall.

Casing is the trim around the door opening. Shapes are available in thicknesses from $^1/_2$ to $^3/_4$ inch and widths varying from $2^1/_4$ to $3^1/_2$ inches. A number of styles are available (fig. 84). Metal casing used at the edge of drywall eliminates the need for wood casing (fig. 79).

Position the casing with about a $^3/_{16}$-inch edge distance from the face of the jamb (fig. 81). Nail with sixpenny or sevenpenny casing or finishing nails, depending on the thickness of the casing. Casing with one thin edge should be nailed with $1^1/_2$-inch brads along the edge. Space nails in pairs about 16 inches apart. Casings with molded forms must have a mitered joint where the head and side casings join (fig. 85A), but rectangular casings are butt-joined (fig. 85B).

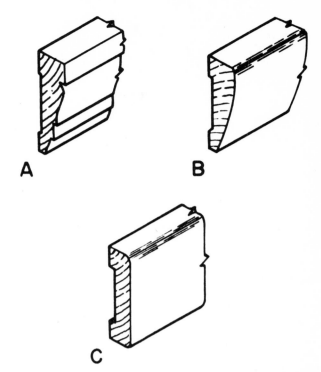

Figure 84.—Styles of door casings: A, colonial; B, ranch; C, plain.

Metal casing can be installed by either of two methods. In one method, the casing is nailed to the door buck around the opening; then the dry wall is inserted into the groove and nailed to the studs in the usual fashion. The other method consists of first fitting the casing over the edge of

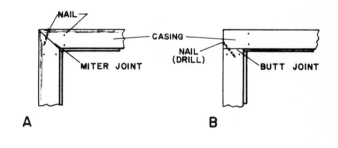

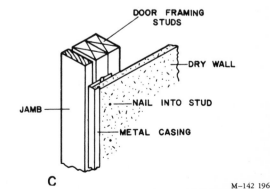

Figure 85.—Installation of door trim: A, molded casing; B, rectangular casing; C, metal casing.

53

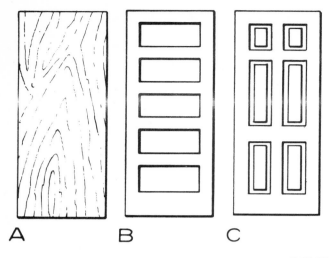

M-135 177

Figure 86.—Interior doors: A, flush; B, five-cross-panel; C, colonial panel type.

the dry wall, positioning the sheet properly, and then nailing through the dry wall and casing into the stud behind (fig. 85C). Use the same type of nails and spacing as for dry wall alone.

Interior doors are either panel or flush type. Flush doors (fig. 86) are usually hollow core. Moldings are sometimes included on one or both faces. Such moldings can also be applied to existing doors where added decoration is desired. The panel-type doors are available in a variety of patterns. Two popular patterns are the five-cross-panel and the colonial.

Standard door height is 6 feet 8 inches; however, a height of 6 feet 6 inches is sometimes used with low ceilings, such as in the upstairs of a story-and-a-half house or in a basement. Framing is limited in hollow-core doors so, if the framing is removed in major cutting to length, that framing must be replaced. Door widths vary, depending on use and personal taste; however, minimums may be governed by building regulations. Usual widths are: (a) Bedroom and other rooms, 2 feet 6 inches; (b) bathroom 2 feet 4 inches; (c) small closet and linen closet, 2 feet.

INSULATION AND MOISTURE CONTROL

INSULATION

The importance of insulation depends upon the climate. Ceiling insulation is beneficial in most climates, although not essential in extremely mild climates where there are neither hot nor cold extremes. Wall insulation is not as essential as ceiling insulation but is required for comfort in cold climates and will pay for itself in heat savings. Floor insulation is also necessary for comfort in the crawl-space house located in a cold climate.

When planning to insulate, consider all major causes of heat loss. Heat loss per unit area through windows and exterior doors is much greater than through most wall materials. Another major heat loss is from air infiltration

around doors and windows. Storm doors and storm windows will reduce air infiltration, and reduce heat transfer by 50 percent or more through the exposed surface. Weatherstrips around doors and windows may result in another major heat saving.

Regardless of type and location of insulation, vapor barriers are required on the warm side of the insulation. Vapor barriers will be discussed in the next section.

Ceiling Insulation

Most houses have an accessible attic with exposed ceiling framing so that any type of insulation can easily be applied. If batt or blanket type is used, get the width that will conform to joist spacing—usually 16 or 24 inches. Loose-fill type could also be used by simply dumping the insulation between joists and screeding it off to the desired thickness (fig. 87). In the northern states with severe winters, at least 6 inches of fill or batt insulation should be used. The same thickness is recommended in the Central States. In the South, thickness of ceiling insulation could be reduced for heating requirements, but cooling requirements may dictate 6 inches or more.

Wall Insulation

Wood-frame walls in existing houses are usually covered both inside and out, so application of batt or blanket insulation is impractical in such renovating. It is possible, however, to blow fill-type insulation into each of the stud spaces. This is done by a contractor equipped for such work. On houses having wood siding, the top strip just below the top plates and strips below each window are removed. Two-inch-diameter holes are cut through the sheathing into each stud space. The depth of each stud space is determined by using a plumb bob, and additional holes are made below obstructions in the spaces. Insulation is forced under slight pressure through a hose and nozzle into the stud space until it is completely filled. Special care should be taken to insulate spaces around doors and windows and at intersections of partition and outside walls.

Stucco, brick, and stone veneer walls can be insulated in a similar manner. The same method can also be used in

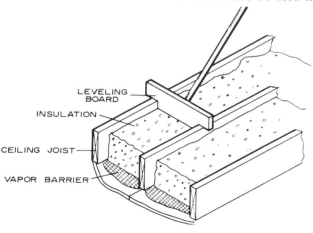

LEVELING BOARD

INSULATION

CEILING JOIST

VAPOR BARRIER

M-135 168

Figure 87.—Installation of loose-fill ceiling insulation.

54

attic and roof spaces that are not accessible for application of other types of insulation.

Solid masonry walls, such as brick, stone, and concrete, can be insulated only by applying insulation to the interior surface. Remember that in doing this some space is being lost. One method of installing such insulation is to adhesively bond insulating board directly to the interior surface. The insulating board can be plastered, left exposed, or covered with any desired finish material. Thicker insulating board can be used for added effectiveness. Another method of installing insulation on the inside surface of masonry walls is through attachment of 2– by 2–inch furring strips to the walls at 16–inch centers and installation of 1–inch blanket insulation between strips. Thicker furring strips would permit use of thicker blanket insulation. The techniques used on masonry walls above grade can also be applied to basement walls.

Floor Insulation

Houses with basements usually do not require insulation under floors because the heating unit warms the basement. The crawl-space house should have an insulated floor in severe climates, and insulated floors will add much to comfort even in moderate climates. Batt-type insulation is often used for floors, although blanket insulation can also

be used. Friction batts fit tightly between joists, and are secured to the bottom side of the subfloor with an adhesive. Batts that are not friction type require some support in addition to the adhesive. This can be provided by wood strips cut slightly longer than the joist space so that they spring into place (fig. 88). They should be about $^3/_{16}$ by $^3/_4$ inch or similar size and spaced 24 to 36 inches apart, or as needed. Another method of supporting floor insulation is by nailing or stapling wire netting between joists. This method can be used for blanket as well as batt type.

VAPOR BARRIERS

Vapor barriers are essential wherever insulation is used. They are always placed near the warm surface and must be continuous over the surface to be effective. Since insulation reduces heat flow, the cold surface of a wall or roof is colder if insulation is used than when the wall is not insulated. This colder surface is likely to be below the dewpoint of the air inside of the house, so condensation occurs.

The common functions of cooking, bathing, laundry, and respiration contribute to moisture inside a house. Additional water vapor may be added by humidifiers operated during the winter. The high vapor pressure inside causes vapor to move out through every available crack and

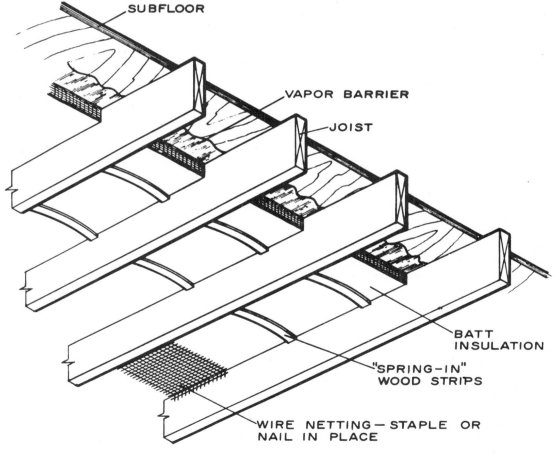

M–135 166

Figure 88.—Installing insulating batts in floor.

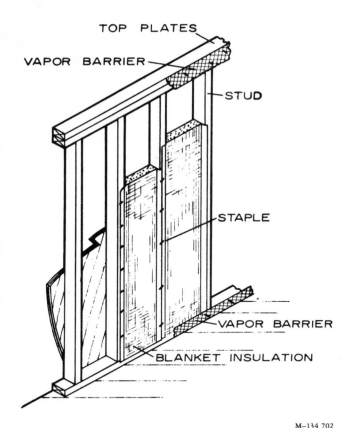

M-134 702

Figure 89.—Installation of blanket insulation with vapor barriers on one side.

even through most building materials. This water vapor condenses in the wall at the point where the temperature is below the dewpoint of the inside atmosphere. The purpose of a vapor barrier is to slow down the rate of vapor flowing into the wall to a rate lower than the outflow to the outside atmosphere.

Continuous Membrane

The most effective vapor barrier is a continuous membrane which is applied to the inside face of studs and joists in new construction. In rehabilitation, such a membrane can be used only where new interior covering materials are to be applied.

The rate of vapor movement through a material is measured in perms. The lower the perm rating of a material, the more effective it is as a vapor barrier. Suitable materials for a membrane are polyethylene 2 mils or more in thickness, asphalt-impregnated and surface-coated kraft papers, and duplex or laminated paper consisting of two sheets of paper cemented together with asphalt.

These vapor barriers can be stapled to furring strips before applying new ceiling or dry wall. If the old ceiling or wall finish is removed, staple the vapor barrier directly to the studs or joists. This type of barrier can also be laid on a subfloor directly under any finish floor or floor covering material. When installing the membrane, be sure to lap all joints at least 2 inches and be careful not to puncture it. Naturally, nail anchorages of finished floor will puncture

the barrier, however, this will not greatly reduce its effectiveness.

Blanket Insulation with Vapor Barrier

Most blanket insulation has a vapor barrier on one side. Place the insulation with the vapor barrier toward the warm surface. Tabs on the blanket must be stapled to the inside face of the stud or joist (fig. 89), and adjacent tabs should lap each other. Tabs stapled to the side of studs or joists in the cavity will be ineffective because vapor will move out between the tabs and framing members. In rehabilitation, this type of vapor barrier can be used only where the old interior covering materials are completely removed or where furring strips are added on the inside. Insulation is installed between furring strips in the same manner as between studs.

Vapor-Resistant Coating

Where loose-fill insulation has been used in walls and ceiling and no new interior covering is planned, a vapor-resistant coating should be applied to the inside surface. One method for applying such a coating is to paint the interior surface of all outside walls with two coats of aluminum primer, which are subsequently covered with decorative paint. This does not offer as much resistance to vapor movement as a membrane, so it should be used only where other types cannot be used. If the exterior wall covering is permeable enough to allow moisture to escape from the wall, a vapor-resistant coating on the inside should be adequate.

Soil Cover

Crawl spaces can be ventilated to effectively remove most moisture, but a soil cover will keep a lot of moisture from ever entering the crawl space. Any of the continuous membranes just mentioned can be used. Lay the membrane so that it contacts the outside walls and has a lap of at least 2 inches at all joints (fig. 90). Use bricks or stones on top of the membrane to hold it down and prevent curling. Ventilation requirements are greatly reduced where a soil cover is used.

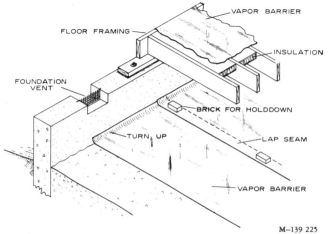

M-139 225

Figure 90.—Vapor barrier for crawl space (ground cover).

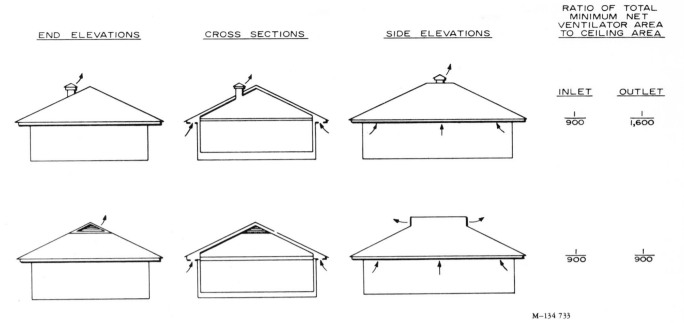

END ELEVATIONS   CROSS SECTIONS   SIDE ELEVATIONS

INLET   OUTLET

$\frac{1}{900}$ $\frac{1}{1,600}$

$\frac{1}{900}$ $\frac{1}{900}$

M–134 733

Figure 91.—Attic ventilation with hip roof.

VENTILATION

Ventilation of attics and crawl spaces is essential in all houses located where the average January temperature is 35° F or lower. Vapor barriers help to control moisture problems, but there are always places, such as around utility pipes, where some moisture escapes. In the older house that does not have proper vapor barriers, ventilation is especially important.

Attic and Roof

Moisture escaping from the house into the attic tends to collect in the coldest part of the attic. Relatively impermeable roofing, such as asphalt shingles or a built-up roof,

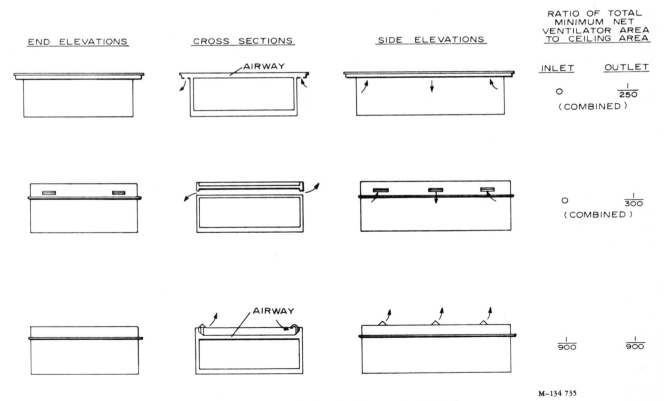

RATIO OF TOTAL
MINIMUM NET
VENTILATOR AREA
TO CEILING AREA

END ELEVATIONS   CROSS SECTIONS   SIDE ELEVATIONS

INLET   OUTLET

AIRWAY

O $\frac{1}{250}$
(COMBINED)

O $\frac{1}{300}$
(COMBINED)

AIRWAY

$\frac{1}{900}$ $\frac{1}{900}$

M–134 735

Figure 92.—Ventilation of ceiling space in flat roof.

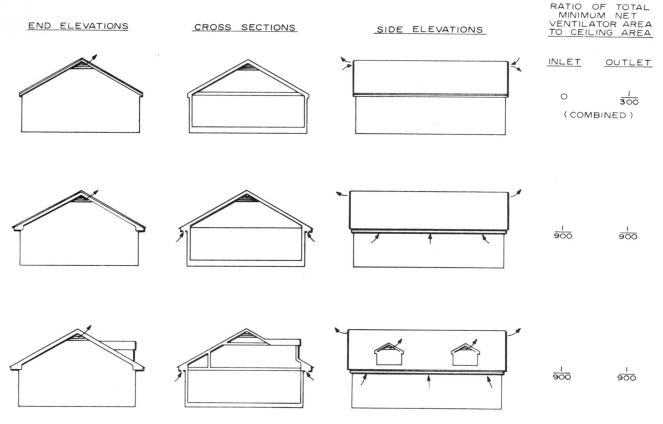

END ELEVATIONS	CROSS SECTIONS	SIDE ELEVATIONS	RATIO OF TOTAL MINIMUM NET VENTILATOR AREA TO CEILING AREA	
			INLET	OUTLET
			O	$\frac{1}{300}$
			(COMBINED)	
			$\frac{1}{900}$	$\frac{1}{900}$
			$\frac{1}{900}$	$\frac{1}{900}$

Figure 93.—Attic ventilation with gable roof.

M–134 734

complicates the problem by preventing the moisture from escaping to the outside. The only way to get the moisture out is to ventilate the attic. Attic ventilation also helps keep a house cool during hot weather.

Where possible, inlet vents should be provided in the soffit area and outlet vents should be provided near the ridge. This results in natural circulation regardless of wind direction. The warm air in the attic rises to the peak, goes out the vents, and fresh air enters through the inlet vents to replace the exhausted air. In some attics only gable vents can be used. Air movement is then somewhat dependent upon wind. The open area of the vent must be larger than where both inlet and outlet vents are provided.

Hip roofs cannot have gable vents near the peak, so some other type of outlet ventilator must be provided (fig. 91). This can be either a ventilator near the ridge, or a special flue provided in the chimney with openings into the attic space. Both types require inlet vents in the soffit area. The hip roof can also be modified to provide a small gable for a conventional louvered vent.

Flat roofs with no attic require some type of ventilation above the ceiling insulation. If this space is divided by joists, each joist space must be ventilated. This is often accomplished by a continuous vent strip in the soffit. Drill through all headers that impede passage of air to the opposite eave. Other methods are illustrated in figure 92.

Cathedral ceilings require the same type of ventilation as flat roofs. A continuous ridge vent is also desirable because

even with holes in the ridge rafter, air movement through the rafter space is very sluggish without a ridge vent. Houses with intersecting roofs or hip roofs create special problems.

Methods of ventilating gable roofs and the amount of ventilation for various types are shown in figure 93. Ratios shown for all ventilation should be multiplied by the total ceiling area to find the size of opening required for the vent. The open area required should be completely unobstructed. Where 16-mesh screen is used to cover the area, the vent area should be doubled.

Crawl Space

An enclosed crawl space under the house floor receives moisture from the soil below. This moisture produces both a decay and termite hazard. To keep the crawl space dry, vents are required with a total free area of not less than $\frac{1}{150}$ of the ground area. This vent area must be divided into four or more openings distributed around the foundation. It is preferable to have one near each corner. If there is a partial basement, the crawl space can be vented to the basement instead of outside. Where a soil cover or a vapor barrier is laid over the entire area of the crawl space, the required ventilation area is greatly reduced. A total free area of only $\frac{1}{1500}$ of the ground area is sufficient. These minimum areas are free areas and must be enlarged when screens or other obstructions are included with the vent.

58

Several types of foundation vents can be purchased commercially for easy installation in the appropriate size opening. Screen sizes vary, depending on whether they are insect-proof or rodent-proof. Manufactured vents usually have a statement of free area. Often it may be sufficient to attach a screen over an opening rather than to purchase a manufactured vent.

INTERIOR ITEMS

RELOCATING PARTITIONS

One of the most common occurrences in remodeling is the moving of partitions for a more convenient room layout. It may mean eliminating a partition or adding a partition in another location.

Removing a Partition

The nonbearing partition is easily removed because none of the structure depends upon it. If the covering material is plaster or gypsum board, it cannot be salvaged, so remove it from the framing in any manner. The framing can probably be reused if it is removed carefully.

The main problem presented by removing a nonbearing partition is the unfinished strip left in the ceiling, wall, and floor. This unfinished strip in the ceiling and wall is easily finished by plastering to the same thickness as the existing plaster or by cutting strips of gypsum board to fit snugly into the unfinished strip and finishing the joints with joint compound and tape. Flooring can also be patched by inserting a wood strip of the same thickness and species as the existing floor. If existing flooring runs parallel to the wall, patching is fairly effective; but where the flooring runs perpendicular to the wall, the patch will always be obvious unless a new floor covering is added. In making the patch, cut the flooring to fit as snugly as possible. Even where the flooring is well fitted and of the same species, it may not be exactly the same color as the existing flooring.

Removing a load-bearing partition involves the same patching of walls, ceiling, and floor as the nonbearing partition but, in addition, some other means of supporting the ceiling joists must be provided. If attic space above the partition is available, a supporting beam can be placed above the ceiling joists in the attic, so that the joists can hang from the beam. The ends of the beam must be supported on an exterior wall, a bearing partition, or a post that will transfer the load to the foundation. Wood hanger brackets are installed at the intersection of the beam with each joist. One method is illustrated in figure 94. This type of support can be installed before the wall is removed, and eliminates the need for temporary support.

Where an exposed beam is not objectionable, it can be installed after the partition is removed. A series of jacks with adequate blocking or some other type of support is required on each side of the partition while the transition between the partition and a beam is being made. The

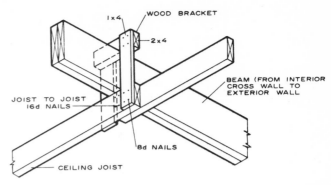

M-135 146

Figure 94.—Framing for flush ceiling with wood brackets.

bottom of the beam should be at least 6 feet 8 inches above the floor.

There may be situations where an exposed beam is undesirable and no attic space is available, as in the ground floor of a two-story house. A beam can be provided in the ceiling with joists framing into the sides of it. Temporary support for the joists is required similar to that used for installing the exposed beam. The joists must be cut to make room for the beam. Install joist hangers on the beam where each joist will frame into it (fig. 95). Put the beam in place and repair the damaged ceiling.

Size of the beam required will vary greatly, depending on beam span, span of joists framing into it, and material used for the beam. Determination of beam size should be made by an engineer or someone experienced in construction.

Adding a Partition

A partition is added by simply framing it in, much as in new construction. Framing is usually done with 2 by 4's, although 2- by 3-inch framing is also considered adequate for partitions. The first step in framing should be to install the top plate. If ceiling joists are perpendicular to the

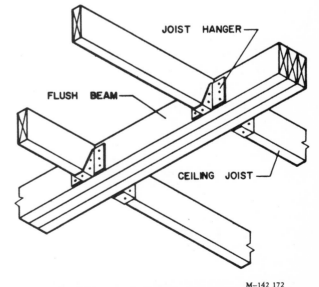

M-142 172

Figure 95.—Flush beam with joist hangers.

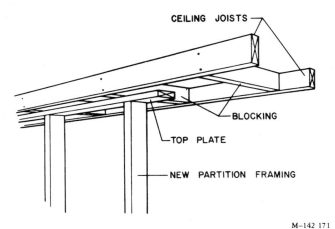

Figure 96.—Blocking between joists to which the top plate of a new partition is nailed.

partition, nail the top plate to each joist using sixteenpenny nails. If ceiling joists are parallel to the partition and the partition is not directly under a joist, install solid blocking between joists at no more than a 2–foot spacing (fig. 96)

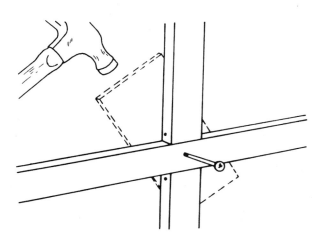

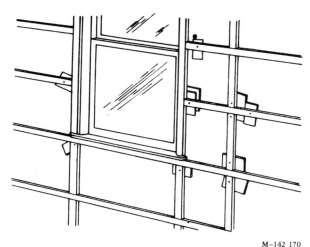

Figure 97.—Shingle shims behind furring to produce a smooth vertical surface.

and nail the top plate to the blocking. To assure a plumb partition hold a plumb bob along the side of the top plate at several points and mark these points on the floor. Nail the sole plate to the floor joists or to solid blocking between joists in the same manner as the top plate was nailed to the ceiling joists. The next step is to install studs to fit firmly between the plates at a spacing of 16 inches. Check the required stud length at several points. There may be some variation. Toenail the studs to the plates, using eightpenny nails. If conditions permit, it may be easier to partially assemble the wall on the floor and tilt it into place. First, the top plate is nailed to the studs and the frame tilted into place, after which studs are toenailed to the bottom plate as above. Frame in doors where desired in the manner described under the section on doors. The partition is then ready for wall finish and trim, which are discussed in the sections which follow.

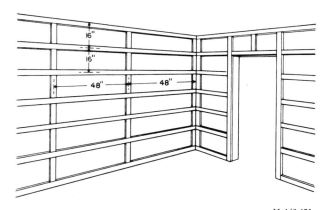

Figure 98.—Application of horizontal furring to interior wall.

INTERIOR WALL FINISH

Minor cracks in plaster or dry wall can be easily patched by filling the crack with a plaster-patching mix and sanding after the plaster dries. A fiberglass fabric applied over the crack helps prevent recurrence. This works well when the cracks are limited in number, but if plaster is generally cracked or pulled loose from its backing, a new covering material should be used.

In houses that require a new wall finish, some type of dry wall sheet material is usually the most practical. The application of most dry wall requires no special tools or skills, and it can be applied in a manner to smooth out unevenness and to cover imperfections. The most common forms of dry wall are gypsum board, plywood, hardboard, fiberboard, and wood paneling. Dry wall is usually applied to framing or to furring strips over the framing or existing wall finish. If the existing wall finish is smooth, new wall finish can sometimes be glued or nailed directly to the existing wall. In this direct application there is no thickness requirement for the new covering because it is continuously supported. For dry wall applied over framing or furring, the recommended thicknesses for 16– and 24–inch spacing of fastening members are listed in the following tabulation:

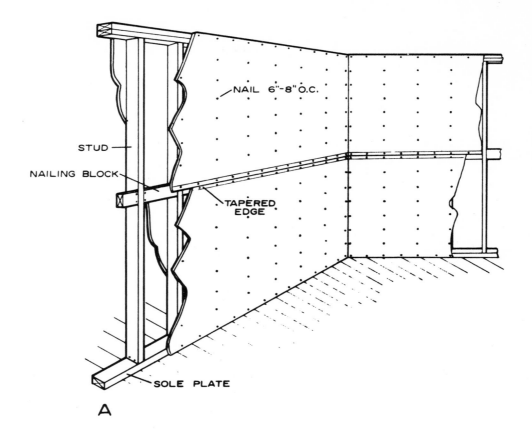

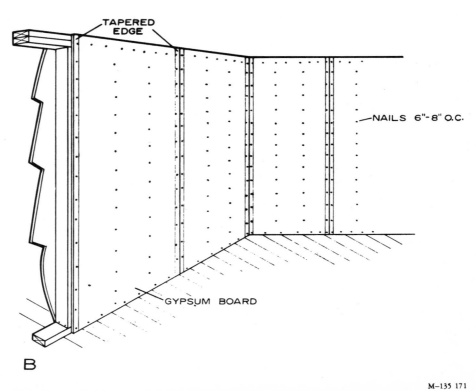

Figure 99.—Installing gypsum board on walls: A, horizontal application; B, vertical application.

M–135 171

Finish	Minimum material thickness (in.) when framing is spaced	
	16 in.	24 in.
Gypsum board	3/8	1/2
Plywood	1/4	3/8
Hardboard	1/4	—
Fiberboard	1/2	3/4
Wood paneling	3/8	1/2

The 1/4-inch plywood or hardboard may be slightly wavy unless applied over 3/8-inch gypsum board.

In order to prepare a room for a new wall finish, first locate each stud. They are usually spaced 16 inches apart and at doors and windows. The easiest way to find them is to look for nailheads in dry wall or baseboard. These nails have been driven into studs. Where there is no evidence of nailheads, tap the wall finish with a hammer. At the stud, the sound will be solid; whereas, the space between studs will sound hollow. Commercial stud finders are also available at hardware and building supply stores. These operate by the use of a magnet that points to nail heads. Mark the stud locations in order to attach horizontal furring strips or to nail on paneling applied without furring strips.

Check walls for flatness by holding a straight 2 by 4 against the surface. Mark locations that are quite uneven. Also check for true vertical alinement by holding a large carpenter's level on the straight 2 by 4 against the wall. As furring is applied, use shingles as shims behind the furring where needed to produce a smooth vertical surface (fig. 97).

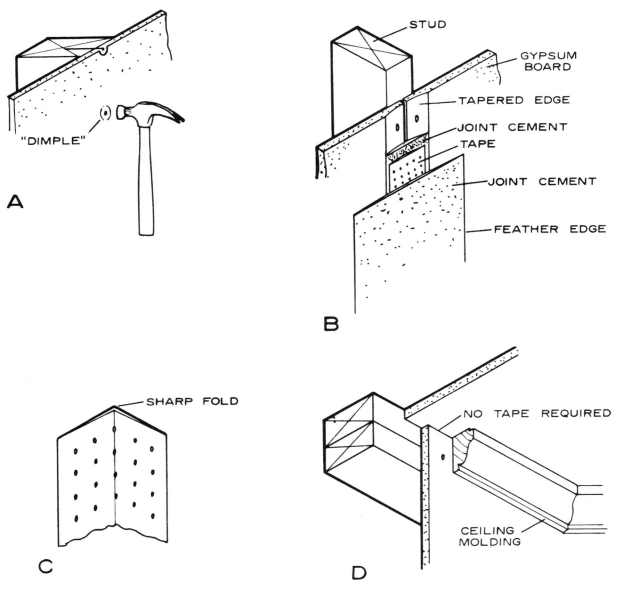

M–134 769

Figure 100.—Preparing gypsum dry-wall sheets for painting: A, drive nails in "dimple" fashion; B, detail of joint treatment; C, corner tape; D, ceiling molding.

Apply standard 1– by 2–inch furring horizontally at 16– or 24–inch spacing, depending on the cover material to be used (fig. 98). Nail the furring at each stud. Remove existing base trim and window and door casings and apply furring around all openings. Also use vertical furring strips where vertical joints will occur in the dry wall.

After this preparation, any of the usual dry wall materials can be applied.

Gypsum Board

Gypsum board is one of the lowest cost materials for interior finish; however, the labor required to finish joints may offset the low material cost. This sheet material is composed of a gypsum filler faced with paper. Recessed edges accommodate tape for joints. Sheets are 4 feet wide and 8 feet long or longer. They can be applied vertically or horizontally. Sheets the entire length of a room can be applied horizontally, leaving only one joint at the mid-height of the wall (fig. 99).

For both horizontal and vertical application, nail completely around the perimeter of the sheet and at each furring strip; for direct application to framing, nail at each stud. Use fourpenny cooler-type nails for $3/8$–inch–thick gypsum board and fivepenny cooler-type nails for $1/2$–inch–thick gypsum board. Space the nails 6 to 8 inches apart. Lightly dimple the nail location with the hammerhead, being careful not to break the surface of the paper. Minimum edge nailing distance is $3/8$ inch. Screws are sometimes used instead of nails.

The conventional method of preparing gypsum sheets for painting includes the use of a joint cement and perforated joint tape. Some gypsum board is supplied with a strip of joint paper along one edge, which is used in place of the tape. After the gypsum board has been installed and each nail driven in a "dimple" fashion (fig. 100A), the walls are ready for treatment. Joint cement ("spackle" compound), which comes in powder or ready-mixed form, should have a soft putty consistency so that it can be easily spread with a trowel or wide putty knife. The gypsum board edges are usually tapered so that, where two sheets are joined, there is a recessed strip to receive joint cement and tape. If a sheet has been cut, the edge will not be tapered. A square edge is taped in much the same manner as the beveled edge except the joint cement will raise the surface slightly at the seam, and edges have to be feathered out further for a smooth finish. Complete instructions are included with taping material. The procedure for taping (fig. 100B) is as follows:

1. Use a wide spackling knife (5 in.) and spread the cement over the tapered and other butt edges, starting at the top of the wall.

2. Press the tape into the recess with the knife until the joint cement is forced through the small perforations.

3. Cover the tape with additional cement to a level surface, feathering the outer edges—allow to dry.

4. Sand lightly and apply a thin second coat, feathering the edges again. A third coat may be required after the second coat has dried.

5. After cement is dry, sand smooth.

6. For hiding nail indentations at members between edges, fill with joint cement. A second coat is usually required. Again sand when dry.

Interior and exterior corners may be treated with perforated tape. Fold the tape down the center to a right angle (fig. 100C). Now (a) apply cement on each side of the corner, (b) press tape in place with the spackle or putty knife, and (c) finish with joint cement and sand when dry. Wallboard corner beads of metal or plastic also can be added to provide strength. Such metal corners are recommended. They are nailed to outside corners and treated with joint cement. The junction of the wall and ceiling can also be finished with a wood molding in any desired shape, which will eliminate the need for joint treatment (fig. 100D). Use eightpenny finishing nails spaced 12 to 16 inches apart and nail into the top wallplate.

Treatment around window and door openings depends on the type of casing used. When a casing head and trim are used instead of a wood casing, the jambs and the beads may be installed before or during application of the gypsum wall finish. These details are covered in the section on "Doors."

Plywood and Hardboard

Plywood and hardboard are usually in 4– by 8–foot sheets for vertical application. However, 7–foot–long panels can sometimes be purchased for use in basements or other low-ceiling areas. Plywood can be purchased in a number of species and finishes with wide variation in cost. Hardboard imprinted with a wood grain pattern is generally less expensive. The better hardboard paneling uses a photograph of wood to provide the woodgrain effect, which produces a very realistic pattern. Both plywood and hardboard can be purchased with a hard, plastic finish that is easily wiped clean. Hardboard is also available with vinyl coatings in many patterns and colors.

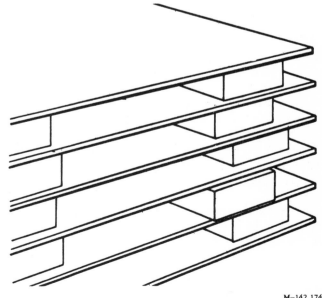

M-142 174

Figure 101.—Stacking panels for conditioning to room environment prior to use.

The plywood or hardboard interior finish material should be delivered to the site well before application to allow the panels to assume conditions of moisture and temperature in the room. Stack the panels, separated by full length furring strips (fig. 101), to allow air to get to all panel faces and backs. Panels should remain in the room at least a couple of days before application.

In applying the panels to the wall, the start depends partly on whether or not the wall corners are truly vertical. If the starting corner is straight, the first panel is merely butted to the corner and subsequent panels located so they lap on studs. If the panel corner or other surface is not truly vertical, place the panel edge on a vertical line 50 inches from the surface, plumb that edge with a carpenter's level, and use an art compass to scribe the outline of the cut to be made on the other edge (fig. 102). Cut the panel and move it against the corner. After the first panel is placed, install successive panels by butting edges against the previous panel, being careful to maintain a true vertical line. Any misalinement is less noticeable, of course, if all walls are paneled. A similar procedure can be used for fitting panels against the ceiling.

Panels can be fastened with nails or adhesive. Adhesive is sometimes preferable because there are no nailheads to mar the finish. Most adhesives include instructions for application, and these instructions should be followed carefully. Use an adhesive that allows enough open assembly time to adjust the panel for a good fit. Where panels are nailed, use small finishing nails (brads). Use $1^1/_2$–inch–long nails for $^1/_4$– or $^3/_8$–inch–thick materials and space 8 to 10 inches apart on edges and at intermediate supports. Most panels are grooved and nails can be driven in these grooves. Set nails slightly with a nail set. Many prefinished materials are furnished with small nails having heads that match the color of the finish; thus no setting is required.

Wood and Fiberboard Paneling

Wood and fiberboard paneling elements are tongued-and-grooved and are available in various widths. Wood is usually limited to no more than 8 inches in nominal width. Fiberboard paneling is often 12 or 16 inches wide. Paneling should also be stacked in the room to be paneled, as recommended for plywood and hardboard, to stabilize at the temperature and moisture conditions of the room. Paneling is usually applied vertically, but at times is applied horizontally for special effects.

Vertically applied paneling is nailed to horizontal furring strips or to nailing blocks between studs. Nail with $1^1/_2$– to 2–inch finishing or casing nails. Blind nail through the tongue, and for 8-inch boards, face nail near the opposite edge. Where 12- or 16-inch-wide fiberboard is used, two face nails may be required. Color-matched nails are sometimes supplied with the fiberboard. Staples may also be used in the tongue of fiberboard instead of nails. Where adhesive is used, the only nailing is the blind nail in the tongue.

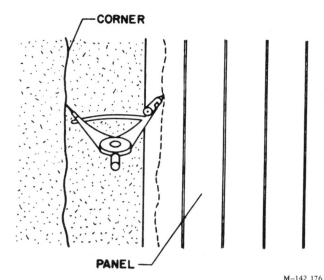

M–142 176

Figure 102.—Scribing of cut at panel edge to provide exact fit in a corner or at ceiling.

CEILINGS

Ceilings can be finished with gypsum board or other sheet materials in much the same manner as interior walls, or a variety of ceiling tiles can be used, including the type for use with suspended metal or wood hangers. The suspended ceiling is particularly useful in rehabilitation of houses with high ceilings. It covers many imperfections, and lowers the ceiling to a more practical height. The space above the new ceiling may be useful for electrical wiring, plumbing, or heating ducts added during rehabilitation, and this mechanical equipment remains easily accessible.

Cracks in plaster ceilings can be repaired with plaster patching in the same manner as walls are patched; however, where cracks are extensive, a new ceiling is the only cure.

Gypsum Board

Gypsum board can be applied directly to ceiling joists by first removing existing ceiling material. It may also be applied directly over plaster or to furring strips nailed over the existing ceiling where plaster is uneven. Use 2– by 2–inch or 2– by 3–inch furring strips oriented perpendicular to the joists and spaced 16 inches on centers for $^3/_8$–inch gypsum board or 24 inches on centers for $^1/_2$–inch gypsum board. Nail the furring strips with two tenpenny nails at each joist. Apply the gypsum boards with end joints staggered and centered on a joist or furring strip. Place the sheets so there is only light contact at joints. One or two braces slightly longer than the ceiling height are quite useful in installing the gypsum sheets (fig. 103). Nail the gypsum board to all supporting members with nails spaced 7 to 8 inches apart. Use fivepenny cooler-type nails for $^1/_2$–inch gypsum board and fourpenny nails for $^3/_8$–inch gypsum board. Nailheads should not penetrate the surface. Each nailhead location should be slightly dimpled with the hammerhead, being careful not to break the surface of the paper. Finish the joints and nailheads in the same manner described under interior wall finish. Where gypsum board is used, it should be applied to the ceiling before wall finish is applied.

Ceiling Tile

Ceiling tile is available in a variety of materials and patterns with a wide range in cost. It can be applied directly to a smooth backing, but the usual application is to furring strips. Suspended ceilings will be discussed in the next section.

If the existing ceiling has a flat surface, tile can be fastened with adhesive. Use an adhesive recommended by the tile manufacturer and follow directions carefully. A small spot of adhesive at each corner and center is usually sufficient. Edged-matched tile can also be stapled if the backing is wood.

A more common method of installing ceiling tile is through fastening them to furring strips. Nominal 1– by 3– or 1– by 4–inch furring strips are used where ceiling joists are spaced no more than 24 inches apart. Nail strips with two sevenpenny or eightpenny nails to each joist. Where trusses or ceiling joists are spaced up to 48 inches apart, use nominal 2– by 2– or 2– by 3–inch furring nailed with two tenpenny nails to each joist. The furring should be a low-density wood, such as the softer pines, if tile is to be stapled to the furring.

Locate the strips by first measuring the width of the room (parallel to joists); place the first furring strip at the center of the room, establish the number of complete courses, and adjust edge spacing so that edge courses are equal in width. Plan spacing perpendicular to joists in the

same manner, so the end courses will be equal. Start at one side and continue across the room, waiting until the last row is being installed to cut the tile for a close fit. Ceiling tile usually has a tongue on two adjacent edges and grooves on the other edges. In installing, keep the tongue edges on the open side so they can be stapled to nailing strips. Use a small finishing nail or adhesive at the edge of the tile next to the wall. Use one staple at each furring strip on the leading edge and two staples along the side (fig. 104). A small finishing nail or adhesive is again required in the edge of the tile against the wall where each row is completed.

In applying the tile, be careful not to soil the surface, as it is usually factory-finished and requires no painting.

Suspended Ceiling

Suspended ceilings consist of a grid of small metal or wood hangers, supported by hanging them from the ceiling framing with wire or strap, and drop-in panels sized to fit the grid system. This type of ceiling can be adjusted to any desired height. Where the existing ceiling is normal height, the hangers can be supported only 2 or 3 inches below the ceiling and still cover any bulging plaster or other unevenness. Where existing ceilings are high, adjust the hangers to the desired ceiling height.

Suspended ceilings are purchased as a system, which assures panels that are compatible with the supporting grid. Detailed instructions for installation are usually supplied by the manufacturer.

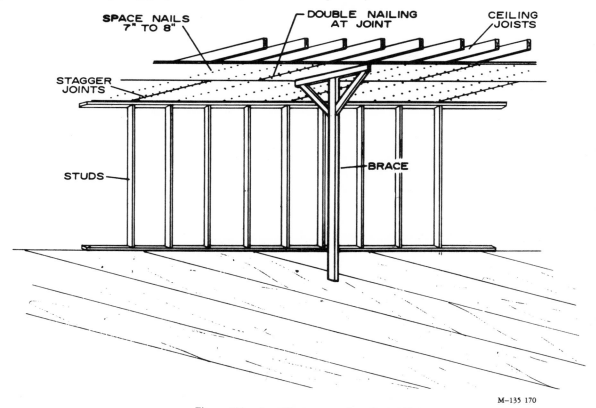

M–135 170

Figure 103.—Installing gypsum board on ceiling.

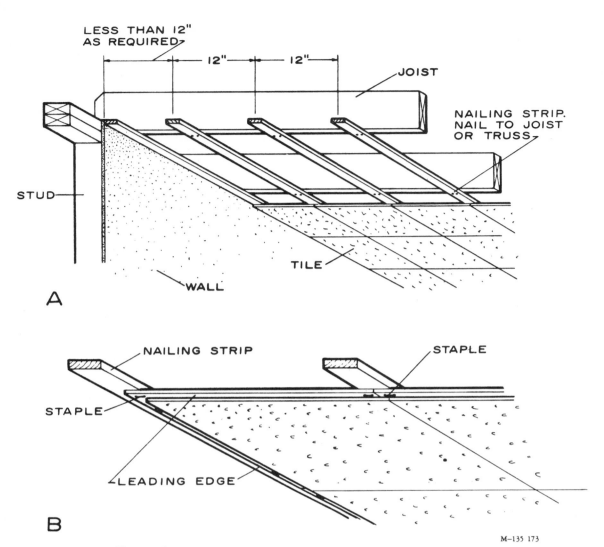

LESS THAN 12"
AS REQUIRED

12"

12"

JOIST

NAILING STRIP.
NAIL TO JOIST
OR TRUSS

STUD

TILE

WALL

A

NAILING STRIP

STAPLE

STAPLE

LEADING EDGE

B

M–135 173

Figure 104.—Ceiling tile installation: A, nailing strip location; B, stapling.

INTERIOR TRIM

Interior trim consists of window and door casings and various moldings. Such trim in existing houses varies considerably, depending on age, style, and quality of the house. The trim found in many older houses is probably no longer on the market, so matching it requires expensive custom fabrication. If the plan is to use existing trim, remove pieces carefully where windows, doors, or partitions are changed, so it can be reused where needed.

Where new trim is planned, the type of finish desired is the basis for selecting the species of wood to be used. For a paint finish, the material should be smooth, close-grained, and free from pitch streaks. Some species that meet these requirements are ponderosa pine, northern white pine, redwood, mahogany, and spruce. The additional qualities of hardness and resistance to hard usage are provided by such species as birch, gum, and yellow-poplar. For a natural finish, the wood should have a pleasing figure, hardness, and uniform color. These requirements are satisfied by species such as ash, birch, cherry, maple, oak, and walnut.

Casing

Casing is the interior edge trim for door and window openings. New casing patterns vary in width from $2^{1}/_{4}$ to $3^{1}/_{2}$ inches and in thickness from $^{1}/_{2}$ to $^{3}/_{4}$ inch. Some common patterns are shown in figure 84. Place the casing with about a $^{3}/_{16}$–inch edge distance from door and window jambs. Nail with sixpenny or sevenpenny casing or finishing nails, depending on thickness of the casing. Space nails in pairs about 16 inches apart, nailing to both jambs and framing. Rectangular casings can be butt-joined at corners (fig. 85B), but molded forms must have a mitered joint (fig. 85A).

Baseboard

Baseboard, the finish between the finished wall and floor, is also available in several sizes and forms (fig. 105). It may be either one or two piece. The two-piece base consists of a baseboard topped with a small base cap which conforms to any irregularities in the wall finish. Most baseboards are finished with a base shoe, except where

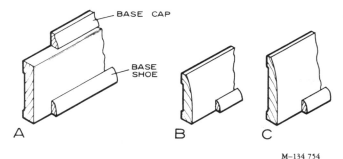

Figure 105.—Baseboard: A, two-piece; B, narrow; C, medium width.

carpet is installed. The base shoe is nailed into the subfloor, so it conforms to irregularities in the finished floor.

Install square-edged baseboard with a butt joint at inside corners and a mitered joint at outside corners. Nail at each stud with two eightpenny finishing nails. Molded base, base cap, and base shoe require a coped joint at inside corners and a mitered joint at outside corners (fig. 106).

Ceiling Moldings

Ceiling moldings are used at the junction of wall and ceiling. They may be strictly decorative where there is a finished joint or they may be specifically for the purpose of hiding a poorly fitted joint. They are particularly useful with wood paneling or other dry wall that is difficult to fit exactly, and where plaster patching cannot be used to finish the joint. Attach the molding with finishing nails driven into the upper wallplates. Large moldings should also be nailed to the ceiling joists.

Miscellaneous Decorative Moldings

Many decorative moldings can be used in a variety of ways. They can be applied to walls or doors to give the effect of relief paneling or carved doors. They can also be used to add interest to existing cabinetwork. Check with a local building supply dealer for available types and ideas on how to use them.

KITCHEN CABINETS

Kitchen cabinets in older houses are often out of style, and may be quite inconvenient in arrangement, type of storage, and workspace provided. New hardware may do much for the appearance of old cabinets. Moldings can be added to achieve the desired character. For a natural finished wood, new doors and drawer fronts can be used on the old cabinet frame. However, it may be best to start over with new cabinets.

Repair of Existing Cabinets

If existing cabinets are adequate and well arranged, certain repairs may be in order. One of the usual problems is latches that no longer operate. These are easily replaced. Presently, one of the popular types is the magnetic catch. The magnetic part is attached to a shelf or the side of the cabinet and a complementary metal plate is attached to the inside face of the door. New door and drawer pulls to match any decor are also easily added.

New door and drawer fronts can be added where more extensive facelifting is desired. All framing can be completely concealed by using flush doors with concealed hinges (fig. 107). Doors are fitted closely edge to edge to give a continuous panel effect. Finger slots in the bottom edge of the door can be used for a simple modern design, or door pulls can be added for any desired character.

Where cabinets are adequate, the one best way to update a kitchen is to apply new counter tops. Custom shops will measure, fabricate, and install them. The most common type is plastic laminate.

Several sheet and roll materials that can be glued to clean, smooth backing are available. These include laminated melamine, laminated polyester, vinyl, and linoleum. They are normally applied to ³/₄-inch exterior-type plywood. Linoleum and vinyl are flexible enough to be shaped to a coved backsplash on the job. Other materials can only be applied flat, so the backsplash is covered

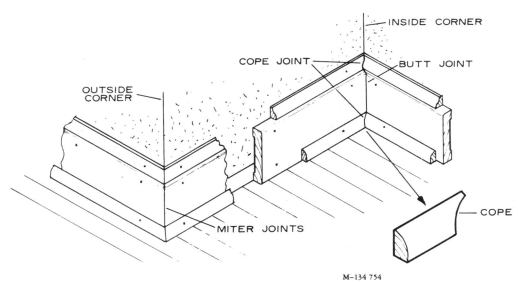

Figure 106.—Installation of base molding.

67

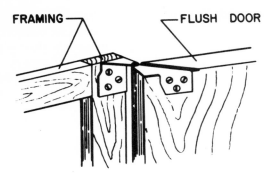

Figure 107.—Concealed hinge used with flush cabinet door.

separately and a metal strip is used to cover the joint between the backsplash and the countertop.

Marble is shop-fabricated and requires no backing material. It must be precut to size in the shop because special tools are required. It is self-edged. There are some objections to marble because of its hardness, and it is expensive, so it is usually limited to bath counters.

Ceramic tile can be set in a mortar bed or applied with adhesive. It is the only material that must be applied at the building site rather than in a shop or factory. It is available in a variety of sizes. The smaller 1–inch–square tile are often preassembled on a mesh backing in 1–foot–square units. It was once very popular and is quite attractive, but is quite hard for kitchen counters and the joints become a maintenance problem.

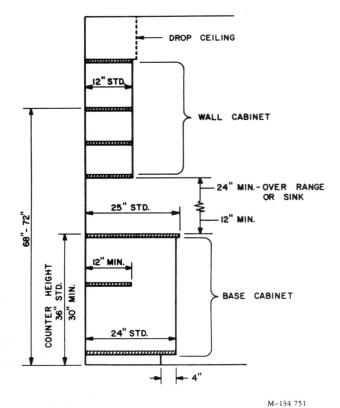

Figure 108.—Kitchen cabinet proportions.

New Cabinets

Kitchen cabinets can be custom made or purchased in units as stock items. Stock cabinets can be purchased in widths varying in 3–inch increments between 12 and 48 inches. These units are fastened to the wall through cleats located at the back of each cabinet. Wall-hung cabinets should be attached with long screws that penetrate into each wall stud.

The range of standard counter heights and depths is shown in figure 108. While a range of sizes is shown, standard counter height is usually 36 inches and counter width is usually 25 inches.

Good kitchen layout is discussed under "Developing the Plan."

CLOSETS

Many older homes are lacking in closet space, and often the closets provided are not well arranged for good usage. Remodeling may involve altering existing closets or adding new ones.

Altering Existing Closets

One thing that can do much to improve closets is to provide fullfront openings to replace small doors. Doors are available in a great variety of widths, particularly accordian doors. Remove wall finish and studs to the width required for a standard accordian-fold or double-hinged door set (fig. 109). Standard double doors may also be suitable. Where the closet wall is load-bearing, use the header sizes listed for window openings. The header can be eliminated for a nonload-bearing wall, and a full ceiling-height accordion-fold door can be used. Frame the opening in the same manner as other door openings, with the rough framed

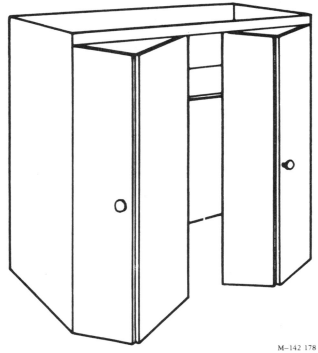

Figure 109.—Double-hinged door set for full-width opening closet.

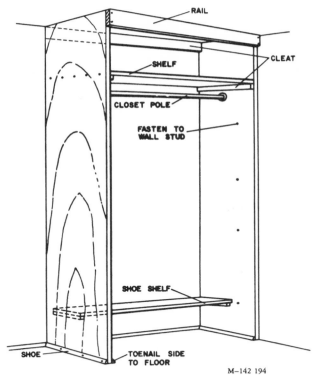

Figure 110.—Wardrobe closet.

opening $2^1/_2$ inches wider than the door or set of doors. Install closet doors in a manner similar to other interior doors. Special types of doors, such as the double-hinged doors, are usually supplied with installation instructions.

Closets can sometimes be made more useful by additions or alterations in shelves and clothes rods. The usual closet has one rod with a single shelf over it. Where hanging space is quite limited, install a second clothes rod about half way between the existing rod and the floor. This type of space can be used for children's clothing or for short items of adult clothing. Shelves can also be added in any manner to fit a particular need. To add either a shelf or a pole, support them by 1– by 4–inch cleats nailed to the end walls of the closet. Nail these cleats with three sixpenny nails at each end of the cleat and at the intermediate stud. Shelf ends can rest directly on these cleats. Attach clothes rods to the cleats that support the shelf.

New Closets

New closets can be built in a conventional manner or wardrobe closets of plywood or particleboard can be built at a lower cost.

Conventional closets are constructed by adding a partition around the closet area, using 2– by 3–inch or 2– by 4–inch framing and gypsum board or other cover material. The method of installing partitions is described under "Adding Partitions." Provide a cased opening for the closet door.

Wardrobe closets require less space because the wall is a single material without framing. Build wardrobe closets as shown in figure 110. Use $^5/_8$– or $^3/_4$–inch plywood or particleboard supported on cleats.

Use a 1– by 4–inch top rail and back cleat. Fasten the cleat to the wall, and in a corner, fasten the sidewall to a wall stud. Toenail base shoe moldings to the floor to hold the bottom of the sidewalls in place. Add shelves and closet poles where desired. Similar units can be built with shelves for linens or other items. Any size or combination of these units can be built. Add plywood doors or folding doors as desired.

SPECIFIC FEATURES

FRAMING FOR UTILITIES

Updating the heating, plumbing, and electrical systems in an older house usually requires a skilled, licensed craftsman, so the details for accomplishing this are not within the scope of this manual. However, certain construction practices are required to accommodate the utilities. Because heating ducts, plumbing stacks and drains, water piping, and electrical conduit must be run throughout the house it is usually difficult to avoid cutting into the structure to accommodate them. Mechanical trades should be cautioned to avoid cutting if possible, and instructed in the manner of cutting where it is unavoidable. At critical points the structure can be altered, but only by or at the direction of someone qualified. Cut members can often be reinforced and any new walls or other framing can be built to accommodate mechanical items.

Cutting Floor Joists

Floor joists must often be cut to accommodate pipe for water supply lines or electrical conduit. This may be in the form of notches at top or bottom of the joist, or as holes drilled through the joist. Notching of joists should be done only in the end quarter of the span and to not more than one-sixth of the depth. If more severe alteration is required, floor framing should be altered. Use headers and tail beams as shown in figure 111 to eliminate the joist at that point.

Holes can also be drilled through joists if the size of hole is limited to 2 inches in diameter and the edges of the hole

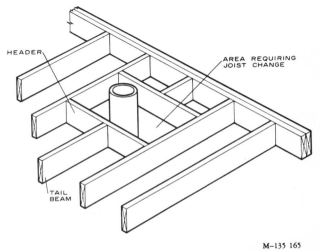

Figure 111.—Headers for joists to eliminate cutting.

69

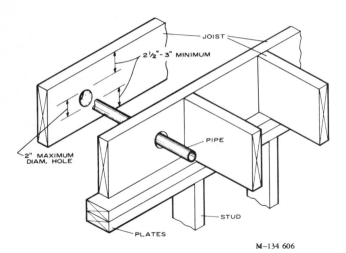

Figure 112.—Boring holes in joists.

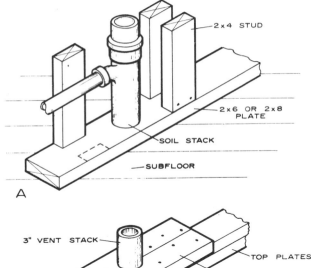

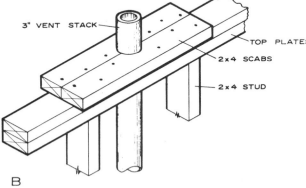

Figure 114.—Framing for vent stack: A, 4-inch soil pipe; B, 3-inch stack vent.

are not less than $2\frac{1}{2}$ inches from the top or bottom of the joist (fig. 112).

Where a joist must be cut and the above conditions cannot be met, add an additional joist next to the cut joist or reinforce the cut joist by nailing scabs to each side.

Bathtub Framing

Where a bathtub is to be added, additional framing may be necessary to support the heavy weight of the tub filled with water. Where joists are parallel to the length of the tub, double the joists under the outer edge of the tub. The other edge is usually supported on the wall framing which also has a double joist under it. Hangers or wood blocks support the bathtub at the enclosing walls (fig. 113).

Utility Walls

Walls containing plumbing stack or vents may require special framing. Four-inch soil stacks will not fit in a standard 2– by 4–inch stud wall. Where a thicker wall is needed, it is usually constructed with 2– by 6–inch top and bottom plates and 2– by 4–inch studs placed flatwise at the edge of the plates (fig. 114A). This leaves the center of the wall open for running both supply and drain pipes through the wall.

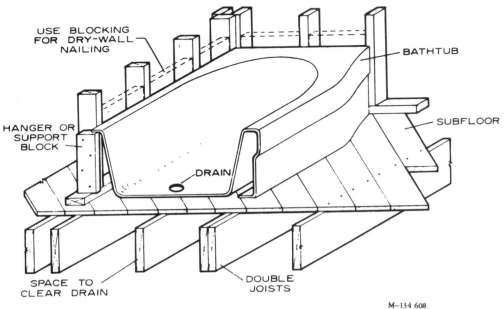

Figure 113.—Framing for bathtub.

70

Three-inch vent stacks do fit into 2– by 4–inch stud walls; however, the hole for the vent requires cutting away most of the top plate. Scabs cut from 2 by 4's are then nailed to the plate on each side of the vent to reinforce the top plate (fig. 114B).

Chimneys and Fireplaces

Defective chimneys and fireplaces are difficult to repair, so it may be best to replace a poor chimney. When gas or oil heaters are used, only small metal vents may be required. Check with local code authorities for type and allowable length of run. These can sometimes be placed in the stud space of an interior partition for low-capacity heaters. Then the defective chimney can be eliminated. If fuels requiring chimneys are used, fabricated metal chimneys can usually be installed at a much lower cost than the conventional masonry chimney. Check local code for requirements for prefabricated chimneys.

Well-built chimneys have flue linings which keep the flue tight even though there are cracks in the masonry. Where flues are not lined, stainless steel flue lining can be installed. This lining can be purchased in 2– or 2–1/2–foot lengths and in cross sections to fit most standard size chimneys. Sections are connected together and inserted from the top, with additional sections being added until the required length is achieved. Note that this type of lining can only be used with a reasonably straight flue. The flue lining will assure safe operation, but cracks in mortar should also be repaired by regrouting.

Fireplaces have several requirements for good draft and smoke-free operation. If they were not built with proper proportions, a metal extension across the top of the fireplace opening will sometimes improve draft. This improvement can be tested by holding a board against the fireplace just above the opening and observing change in draft. Draft can sometimes be improved by extending the height of flue or adding a chimney cap for venturi action. Another possible solution where draft is inadequate is to install a fan in the chimney for forced exhaust.

In cold climates, a damper that can be closed when the fireplace is not in use is quite important. Where there is no damper, an asbestos board can be cut to fit the flue opening at the top of the fireplace and supported on some type of brackets. It would have to be completely removed when the fireplace is in use, which is slightly inconvenient; but it would eliminate heat loss or cold drafts from the flue.

If a new fireplace is desired, professional help is usually required. However, prefabricated metal fireplaces are available which require no special skills for installation. They can be placed on the conventional floor without a separate foundation, and no masonry work is required. Fireplace liners are also available which only require masonry added around them. They require a complete foundation and separate chimney the same as a conventional fireplace, but they are a convenient guide for assuring proper proportions.

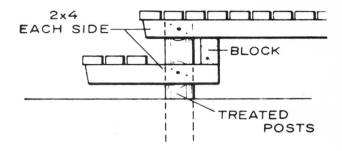

M-135 191

Figure 115.—Single porch step supported on a treated post.

PORCHES

If examination of the porch showed all parts to be in a generally deteriorated condition, complete removal and replacement is recommended. However, it may be feasible to replace components, such as steps, floor, posts, or roof, where other components are in good condition.

Steps

When wood steps are used, the bottom step and carriage should not be in contact with soil. A concrete step can be cast on the ground to support the carriage or it can be supported on a treated wood post. Apply a water-repellent preservative to all wood used in the steps.

If only one step is required and treated posts are used for support, the step can be supported on the same post that supports the edge of the porch (fig. 115). Use treated posts of 5– to 7–inch diameter embedded in the soil at least 3 feet. Nail and bolt the crossmember to the post, and block the inner end to the floor framing with a short 2 by 4.

Where more steps are required, use a 2 by 12 stringer at each end of the steps with the lower end of each stringer

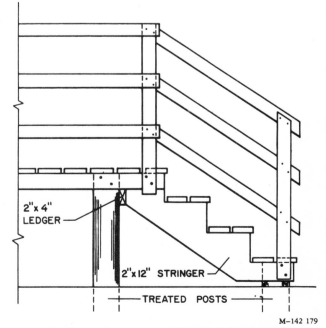

M-142 179

Figure 116.—Step stringer supported by porch framing and posts.

71

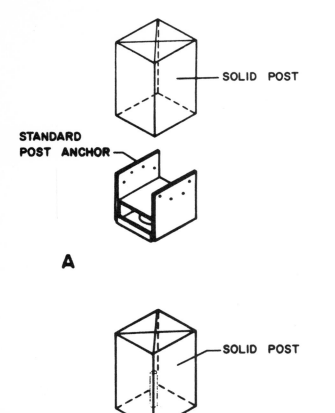

A

STANDARD POST ANCHOR

SOLID POST

STEEL PIN

GALVANIZED WASHER

SOLID POST

CONCRETE FLOOR

B

M–142 180

Figure 117.—Base for post: A, standard post anchor for resistance to uplift; B, galvanized washer and pin where resistance to uplift is not critical.

bolted to a treated post (fig. 116). The upper end can be attached to the porch framing. Concrete or masonry piers can be used in place of treated posts. The important thing is that the stringer be kept from contact with the soil.

Floor

If floor framing is decayed, it should be completely replaced, and all replacement members should be treated with a water-repellent preservative. Framing members should be at least 18 inches above the ground, and good ventilation should be provided under the porch. Framing should be installed to give the finished floor an outward slope of at least $1/8$ inch per foot.

Porch flooring is 1- by 4-inch lumber, dressed and matched. It is blind-nailed at each joist in the same manner as regular flooring. Apply a good stain or deck paint as soon as possible after installation.

Posts

Where a post rests directly on the porch floor, the base of the post may be decayed. The best solution may be to replace the post. When this is done, provide some way to support the post slightly above the porch floor. Standard post anchors can be purchased for this purpose (fig. 117A). Another way to accomplish this is by using a small $3/8$– or $1/2$–inch–diameter pin and large galvanized washer. Drill a hole for the pin in the end of the post and a matching hole in the floor (fig. 117B). Apply a mastic calk to the area and position with the pin inserted and the washer between the post and the floor. This will allow moisture to evaporate from the end of the post and prevent decay. This pinned method should be used only on small porches that will not have a major wind uplift load.

If the existing porch posts are ornamental, it may be desirable to cut off the decayed portion near the base and save the good portion. Perhaps a base slightly larger than the post can be added to replace the decayed portion (fig. 118). Some method of ventilating the base of the post should be provided to avoid further decay. One solution is to use a pin and large washer, as described above for a new post.

Roof

A porch roof can be repaired in much the same manner as repairing the house roof. The difference may be that porch roofs frequently have a very low slope and are often covered with roll roofing. Simply apply an underlayment of asphalt-saturated felt and follow with mineral surfaced half-lap roll roofing applied in accordance with manufacturer's instructions. Use a ribbon of asphalt roof cement or lap seal material under the lapped edge, and avoid using any exposed nails. Extend the roofing beyond the facia enough to form a natural drip edge.

If wood or asphalt shingles are used on the porch roof, apply them as described in the section on "Roofs."

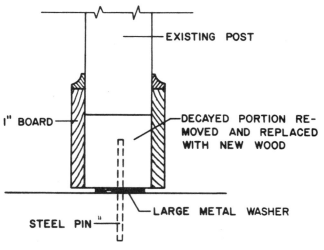

EXISTING POST

1" BOARD

DECAYED PORTION RE-MOVED AND REPLACED WITH NEW WOOD

STEEL PIN

LARGE METAL WASHER

M–142 181

Figure 118.—Replacement of decayed end of porch post.

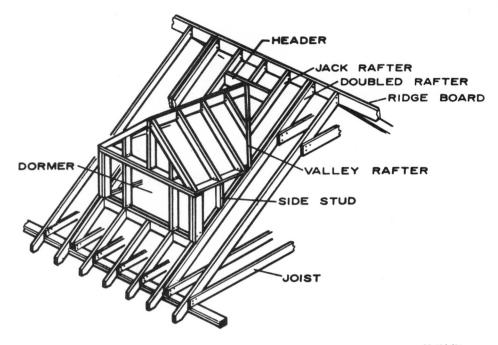

Figure 119.—Framing for gable dormer.

M–134 631

ADDITIONAL SPACE

ATTIC

Making an attic usable may be a simple matter of installing finish ceiling, wall, and floor covering; however, it will often require adding a shed or gable dormer for more space or for natural light and ventilation. Furthermore, the existing joists may not be adequate to support a floor load. It may be best to get professional advice on this unless tables are available that show allowable joist and rafter spans. If the joists are inadequate, the best solution is usually to double existing joists.

Gable Dormer

Where light and ventilation are the main requirements rather than additional space, gable dormers are often used. They are more attractive in exterior appearance than shed dormers but, due to the roof slope, they are usually limited to a small size. They are also more complicated to build then shed dormers.

The roof of the gable dormer usually has the same pitch as the main roof of the house. The dormer should be located so that both sides are adjacent to an existing rafter (fig. 119). The rafters are then doubled to provide support for the side studs and short valley rafters. Tie the valley rafter to the roof framing at the roof by a header. Frame the window and apply interior and exterior covering materials, as described under other appropriate sections.

One of the most critical items in dormer construction is proper flashing where the dormer walls intersect the roof of

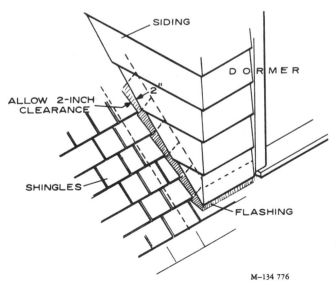

Figure 120.—Flashing at dormer walls.

M–134 776

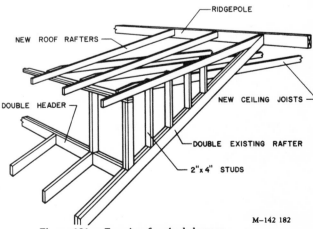

Figure 121.—Framing for shed dormer.

M–142 182

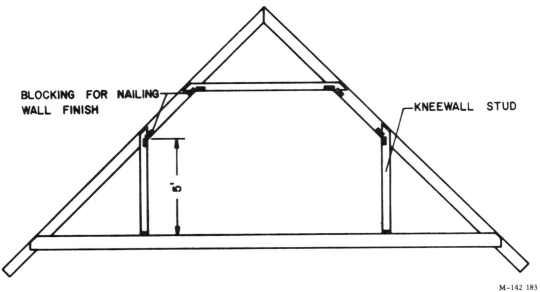

KNEEWALL STUD

5'

M-142 183

Figure 122.—Installation of knee walls and blocking.

the house (fig. 120). When roofing felt is used under the shingles, it should be turned up the wall at least 2 inches. Shingle flashing should be used at this junction. This consists of tin or galvanized metal shingles bent at a 90° angle to extend up the side of the wall over the sheathing a minimum of 4 inches. Use one piece of flashing at each shingle course, lapping successive pieces in the same manner as shingles. Apply siding over the flashing, allowing about a 2-inch space between the bottom edge of the siding and the roof. Cut ends of siding should be treated with water-repellent preservative.

Shed Dormer

Shed dormers can be made any width, and are sometimes made to extend across the entire length of the house. They are less attractive than gable dormers and, for this reason, are usually placed at the back of the house. Sides of the shed

dormer are framed in the same manner as the gable dormer, so the sides should coincide with existing rafters. The low-slope roof has rafters framing directly into the ridgepole (fig. 121). Ceiling joists bear on the outer wall of the dormer, with the opposite ends of the joists nailed to the main roof rafters. The low slope of the dormer roof means that requirements of roofing application will be different from those of the main roof. Shingle sizes and exposures should conform to those shown in table 4.

Knee Walls

Sides of the attic rooms are provided by nailing 2– by 4– or 2– by 3–inch studs to each rafter at a point where the stud will be at least 5 feet long (fig. 122). Studs should rest on a soleplate in the same manner as other partitions. Nail blocking between studs and rafters at the top of the knee wall to provide a nailing surface for the wall finish.

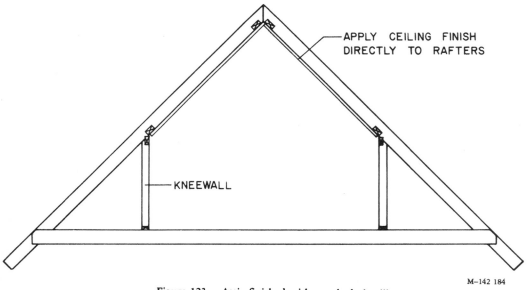

APPLY CEILING FINISH DIRECTLY TO RAFTERS

KNEEWALL

M-142 184

Figure 123.—Attic finished with a cathedral ceiling.

Ceiling

Nail collar beams between opposite rafters to serve as ceiling framing (fig. 122). These should be at least 7¹/₂ feet above the floor. Nail blocking between collar beams and between rafters at their junction to provide a nailing surface for the finish wall and ceiling materials.

An alternate method of installing the ceiling is to eliminate the collar beams and apply the ceiling finish directly to the rafters (fig. 123). This result is in what is commonly called a cathedral ceiling. If the dormer is wide, cross partitions or some other type of bracing is required for stability.

Chimney

If a chimney passes through the attic, it must either be hidden or worked into the decor. Never frame into the chimney. Keep all framing at least 2 inches from the chimney. Where framing is placed completely around the chimney, fill the space between the chimney and framing with noncombustible insulation.

BASEMENT

Basements can be finished to any desired quality, depending on the investment required and the use to be made of the finished space. This may vary from insulated walls with quality paneling, wood floors, and acoustical ceiling, to merely painting the existing concrete walls and floors. Keep in mind that basement areas, even where the grade is low, tend toward dampness thus requiring dehumidification, and tend to be cooler so the rooms may be uncomfortably cool in periods of light heating. A small amount of auxiliary electric heat can partially correct this. Insulation of below-grade concrete or masonry walls is very important.

Floors

If a concrete floor is dry most of the year, it indicates that a vapor barrier was probably applied under the slab at the time it was constructed. In such a basement, resilient tile or indoor-outdoor carpeting could be applied directly to the smooth slab. Any protrusions from the slab should be chipped off. Extension unevenness in the slab indicates that an underlayment over sleepers should be used as a base for the tile or carpet. Install the tile as described under the section on "Floors," following the manufacturer's recommendations on adhesives and installation practices. Carpeting is usually just cut to size and laid flat without special installation except for double-faced tape at edges and seams.

A very low-cost floor can be achieved by merely applying a deck paint. It should be a latex paint to avoid chipping or peeling. Although painting may not give the finished

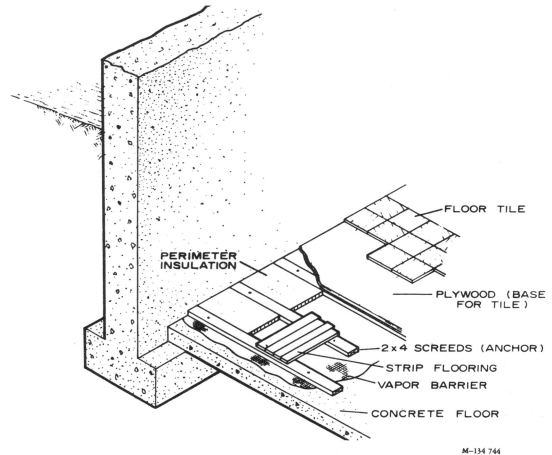

M-134 744

Figure 124.—Installation of wood floors in a basement.

75

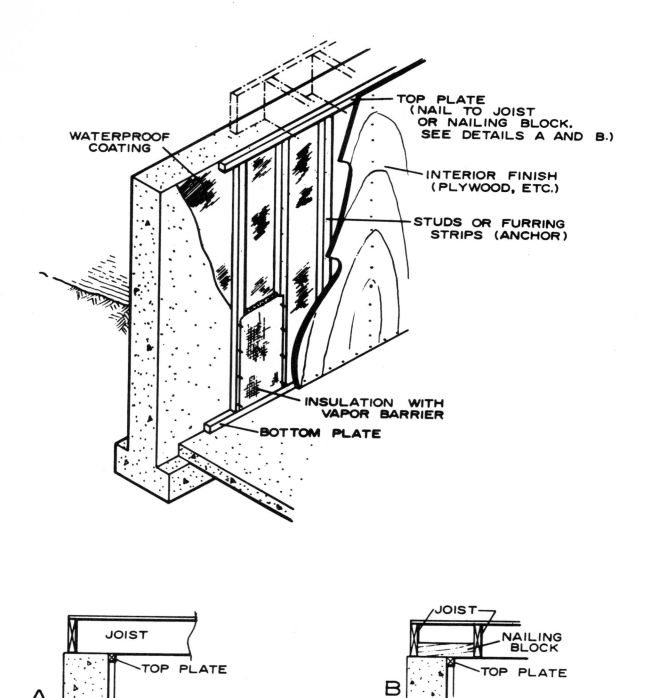

WATERPROOF COATING

TOP PLATE
(NAIL TO JOIST
OR NAILING BLOCK.
SEE DETAILS A AND B.)

INTERIOR FINISH
(PLYWOOD, ETC.)

STUDS OR FURRING
STRIPS (ANCHOR)

INSULATION WITH
VAPOR BARRIER

BOTTOM PLATE

JOIST

TOP PLATE

A

JOIST

NAILING
BLOCK

TOP PLATE

B

M–134 705

Figure 125.—Basement wall finish over framing.

appearance provided by a floor covering, it does brighten the basement and produces a smooth surface that is easily cleaned. It is particularly suited to shops, utility rooms, and playrooms.

Where a concrete floor is desired, but the existing floor is cracked and uneven or damp, a vapor barrier can be laid over the existing floor and a 2– to 3–inch topping of concrete fill can be added.

Where a vapor barrier is required and finished flooring is planned, apply an asphalt mastic coating to the concrete

floor, followed by a good vapor barrier. This can serve as a base for tile; however, the use of furring strips with finish floor applied over them may produce a better end result. Wood flooring manufacturers often recommend that preparation for wood strip flooring consist of the following steps:

1. Mop or spread a coating of tar or asphalt mastic on the concrete, followed by an asphalt felt paper.

2. Lay 2 by 4's flatwise in a coating of tar or asphalt, spacing the rows about 12 inches apart; start at one wall and end at the opposite wall.

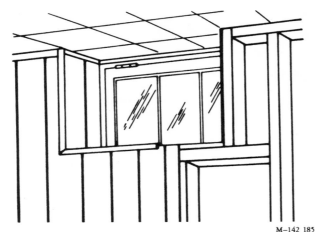

Figure 126.—Framing around basement window of a wall finish application.

3. Place a 2–foot width of insulation around the perimeter, between 2 by 4's, where the outside ground level is near the basement floor elevation.

4. Install wood-strip flooring across the 2 by 4's.

A variation of this preparation for flooring consists of laying a good-quality vapor barrier directly over the slab and anchoring the furring strips to the slab with concrete nails (fig. 124). Insulation and strip flooring are then applied in the same manner described above.

Plywood, $1/2$ or $5/8$ inch thick, can also be applied over furring strips to provide a base for resilient tile or carpet (fig. 124).

Walls

Where basement walls were waterproofed on the outside, there should be no problem in applying most any kind of wall finish. However, if there is any possibility of water entry, it is important to apply a waterproof coating to the inner surface. Numerous coatings of this type are available commercially. These coatings usually cannot be applied over a wall that has previously been painted. Walls can simply be painted for a bright, clean appearance where a more finished appearance is not as essential. If a better interior finish is desired, it is applied over furring strips or rigid insulation.

Furring strips, 2 by 2 inches or larger, are used at the walls in preparation for for the interior finish (fig. 125). Strips should be pressure treated for decay resistance, especially if the walls are not waterproofed. Anchor a 2– by 2–inch bottom plate to the floor at the junction of the wall and floor. Fasten a 2– by 2–inch or larger top plate to the bottom of the joists above (fig. 125A), to nailing blocks (fig. 125B), or to the wall. Then fasten 2– by 2–inch or larger furring strips, at 16– or 24–inch spacing, vertically

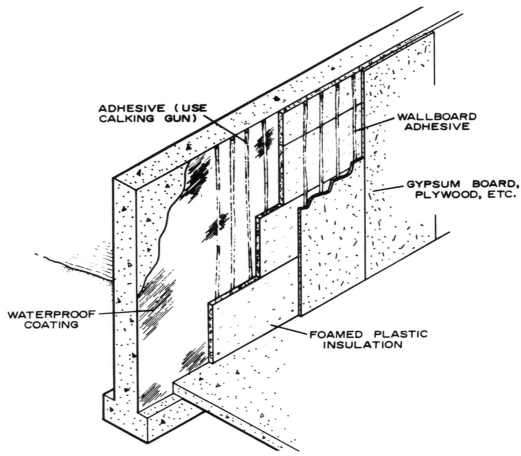

Figure 127.—Basement wall finish over rigid insulation.

between top and bottom plates. Concrete nails are sometimes used to anchor the center of the furring strips to the basement wall.

Before proceeding any further with the finish wall, install all required electrical conduit and outlet boxes between furring strips. Place blanket-type insulation with vapor barrier on the inside face in each space between furring strips. Frame around windows, as shown in figure 126. The wall is then ready to receive the interior finish. Almost any dry-wall material can be applied in the manner described under "Interior Wall Finish."

Wall finish material is sometimes applied over foamed plastic insulation, which is applied directly to basement walls without the use of furring strips. For this method, walls must be smooth and level without protrusions so the sheets of foam insulation can be secured to the walls with beads of adhesive. Use dry wall adhesive to secure the wall finish to the insulation (fig. 127). Follow manufacturer's recommendations on adhesives and methods of installation for both the foam insulation and the dry wall. Select a foam insulation with good vapor resistance to eliminate the need for a separate vapor barrier.

Basement partitions are made in much the same manner as on the main floor. The only difference is in securing the soleplate to the slab with concrete nails or other types of concrete anchors.

Finishing walls should include concealing unsightly items such as steel beams and columns and exposed piping. These items can be covered by building a simple box around them and paneling over the box (fig. 128).

Ceilings

The ceiling finish can be applied using the same materials and techniques described in the section on "Ceilings." In many basements, a suspended ceiling system will be best. It can be placed below piping and electrical conduit, and panels are easily removed for repair or changes in utilities. In considering the use of a suspended ceiling, make certain that at least 7 feet will still be available from floor to ceiling. It may be necessary to apply the ceiling directly to the bottom of floor joists and box around or paint to match the ceiling.

Before installing any ceiling, insulate cold-water pipes. When the basement has a high relative humidity, water condenses on the cold pipes and this condensation drips down on the ceiling where it is under the pipes. Molded insulation that can be fitted over the pipe is commercially available. Commercial insulations are made specifically for wrapping around pipe.

GARAGE

The garage that was built integrally with the house can be used as living space simply by insulating it and adding floor, wall, and ceiling finish. There may be some additional requirement for windows and for heating.

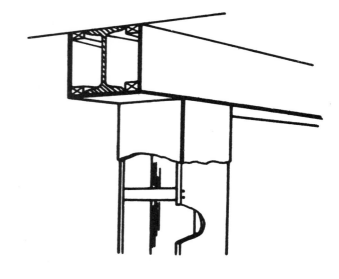

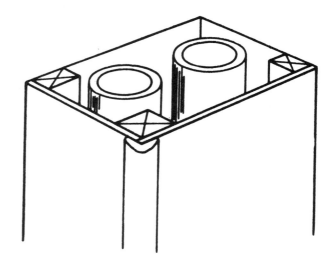

M–142 145

Figure 128.—Application of paneling to cover columns, beams, and pipes.

Floors

The new finish floor is applied directly over the existing concrete slab, or, where headroom is sufficient, over new floor framing above the slab. Where the ceiling of the finished garage is at the same elevation as the house ceiling, new floor framing can be installed to place the new floor at the same level as the house floor. The framing may rest on the foundation wall or be supported on ledgers nailed to the wall studs (fig. 129). Consult joist tables to determine the correct size for the required span. The floor is merely installed as a conventional floor, described under "Floor System," and insulated in the same manner as a crawl-space house, as described under "Insulation."

The garage roof is often lower than the house roof, so that the floor must be placed directly on the concrete slab one or two steps below the house floor. Finish floor can be installed using the same materials and techniques as for a basement slab. If the garage floor is near ground level, insulation is required. If the finished floor is on sleepers over the concrete, place insulation between sleepers.

Another method of insulating is to dig the soil way from the foundation and apply rigid insulation to the outer face of the foundation wall to the depth of the footing (fig. 130). It must be a moisture-proof insulation, such as polystyrene or polyurethane, and should be attached with a mastic recommended by the insulation manufacturer. The insulation should be covered with a material suitable for underground use, such as asbestos-cement board or preservative-treated plywood. Where subterranean termites are a threat, soil can be poisoned (see p. 26) during the backfill.

Walls

The garage walls are not usually insulated, so blanket insulation with a vapor barrier on the inside face should be installed in the space between studs. Then apply any type of dry wall in the manner described under "Interior Wall Finish."

Frame any additional doors and windows following the instructions given under "Doors" and "Windows." It may be convenient to use the existing garage door opening for a sliding glass door, or a window wall. If it is not to be used for either purpose, fill it in, using conventional 2– by 4– inch framing, and install covering materials.

Ceiling

The ceiling can be installed as described under "Ceilings." Be sure to insulate well and ventilate the attic space.

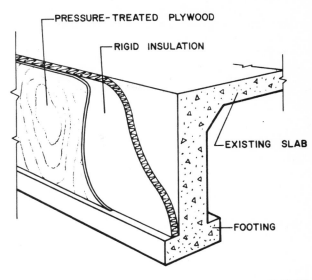

M–142 187

Figure 130.—Application of insulation to outer face of garage foundation wall.

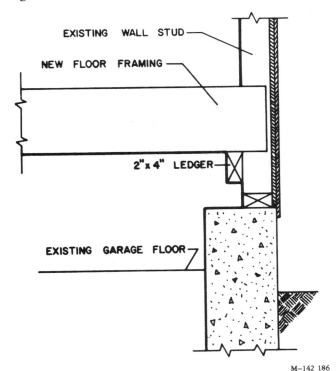

M–142 186

Figure 129.—Framing to bring new garage floor to the level of the house floor.

ADDITIONS

Additions to existing houses are made by employing new construction techniques, and building to match or blend with the existing structure. Previous sections have described methods for installing windows, doors, and covering materials. Most of these instructions also apply to new construction such as in an addition. The main item peculiar to additions is making the connection between the addition and the existing structure.

Where the addition is to be made by extending the length of building, the structure as well as the siding and roofing must match the existing portion. To accomplish this, a complete roofing job may be necessary. Where existing shingles can be matched, some of the shingles near the end must be removed in order to lap the saturated felt underlayment. The new shingles are then worked into the existing shingle pattern. Short pieces of lap siding must also be removed so the new siding can be toothed into the existing siding with end joints offset rather than as one continuous vertical joint.

If the addition is to be perpendicular to the house, the siding can either match or contrast with the existing siding. However, the roofing material should match. Siding at intersection of walls is applied with a corner strip as shown in figure 55.

PAINTING AND FINISHING

Painting and finishing of the house being rehabilitated will usually include repainting or refinishing of existing surfaces as well as providing a finish over new siding, interior wall surfaces, floors, and trim. The exterior finishes are required for appearance and protection from weathering; interior finishes are primarily for appearance, wear resistance, and ease of maintenance of the surface.

WOOD PROPERTIES AND FINISH DURABILITY

The durability of an exterior finish is materially affected by the wood characteristics. Woods that are high in density (heavy), such as dense hardwoods, will be more difficult to finish effectively than lightweight woods. Western redcedar and redwood are two species that have the desired qualities in a high degree.

The amount and distribution of summerwood (darker grained portions) on the surface of softwood lumber also influence the success of the finishing procedure. Finishes, particularly paints, will last longer on surfaces with a low proportion of summerwood.

The manner in which lumber is sawn from the log has an influence on its finishing characteristics. Paint-type and film-forming finishes always perform best on vertical-grain lumber because the summerwood is better distributed on the surface and because vertical-grain lumber is low in swelling across the width of the board.

All woods shrink or swell as they lose or absorb water. Species which shrink and swell the least are best for painting. Checking and warping of wood, and paint peeling are more likely to be critical on woods which are hard, dense, and high in swelling.

Wood that is free of knots, pitch pockets, and other defects is the preferred base for paints, but these defects have little adverse effect on penetrating-type finishes. Smoothly planed surfaces are best for paint finishes, while rougher or sawn surfaces are preferred for penetrating (non-film-forming) finishes.

EXTERIOR FINISHES

Unfinished Wood

Permitting the wood to weather naturally without protection of any kind is, of course, very simple and economical. Wood fully exposed to all elements of the weather, rain and sun being the most important, will wear away at the approximate rate of only $1/4$ inch in a century. The time required for wood to weather to the final gray color will depend on the severity of exposure. Wood in protected areas will be much slower to gray than wood fully exposed to the sun on the south side of a building. Early in the graying process, the wood may take on a blotchy appearance because of the growth of micro-organisms on the surface. Migration of wood extractives to the surface also will produce an uneven and unsightly discoloration, particularly in areas that are not washed by rain.

Unfinished lumber will warp more than lumber protected by paint. Warping varies with the wood density, width and thickness of the board, basic wood structure, and species. Warp increases with density and the width of the board. The width of boards should not exceed eight times the thickness. Flat-grain boards warp more than vertical-grain lumber. Baldcypress, the cedars, and redwood are species which have only a slight tendency to warp.

Water-Repellent-Preservative Finishes

A simple treatment of an exterior wood surface with a water-repellent preservative markedly alters the natural weathering process. Most pronounced is the retention of a uniform natural tan color in the early stages of weathering and a retardation of the uneven graying process which is produced by the growth of mildew on the surface.

Water-repellent finishes generally contain a preservative (usually pentachlorophenol), a small amount of resin, and a very small amount of a water repellent that is frequently wax or waxlike in nature. The water-repellency imparted by the treatment greatly reduces the tendency toward warping, and excessive shrinking and swelling which lead to splitting. It also retards the leaching of extractives from the wood and staining from water at ends of boards.

This type of finish is quite inexpensive, easily applied, and very easily refinished. Water-repellent preservatives can be applied by brushing, dipping, and spraying. Rough surfaces will absorb more solution than smoothly planed surfaces and the treatment will be more durable on them. It is important to thoroughly treat all lap and butt joints and ends of boards. Many brands of effective water-repellent preservatives are on the market.

The initial applications may be short lived (1 yr), especially in humid climates and on species that are susceptible to mildew, such as sapwood and certain hardwoods. Under more favorable conditions, such as on rough cedar surfaces which will adsorb large quantities of the solution, the finish will last more than 2 years.

When blotchy discolorations of mildew start to appear on the wood, remove blotches and rain spatters, and lighten dark areas by steel brushing with the grain. Retreat the surface with water-repellent-preservative solution. If extractives have accumulated on the surface in protected areas, clean these areas by mild scrubbing with a detergent of trisodium-phosphate solution.

The continued use of these water-repellent-preservative solutions will effectively prevent serious decay in wood in above-ground installation. This finishing method is recommended for all wood species and surfaces exposed to the weather.

Only aluminum or stainless steel nails will prevent discoloration on the siding. Galvanized nails will show light stains after several years. Steel nails without rust-resistant treatment should not be used.

Penetrating Pigmented Stain Finishes

The penetrating stains also are effective and economical finishes for all kinds of lumber and plywood surfaces. They are especially well suited for rough-sawn, weathered, and textured wood and plywood. Knotty wood boards and other lower quality grades of wood which would be difficult to paint can be finished successfully with penetrating stains.

These stains penetrate into the wood without forming a continuous film on the surface. Because these is no film or coating, there can be no failure by cracking, peeling, and blistering. Stain finishes are easily prepared for refinishing and easily maintained.

The penetrating pigmented stains form a flat and semi-transparent finish. They permit only part of the wood-grain pattern to show through. A variety of colors can be achieved including shades of brown, green, red, and gray. The only color which is not available is white. This color can be provided only through the use of white paint.

Stains are quite inexpensive and easy to apply. To avoid the formation of lap marks, the entire length of a course of siding should be finished without stopping. Only one coat is recommended on smoothly planed surfaces, where it will last 2 to 3 years. After refinishing, however, the second coat will last 6 to 7 years because the weathered surface has adsorbed more of the stain than the smoothly planed surface.

Two-coat staining is possible on rough-sawn or weathered surfaces, but both coats should be applied within a few hours of each other. When using a two-coat system, the first coat should never be allowed to dry before the second is applied, because this will seal the surface and prevent the second coat from penetrating. A finish life of up to 10 years can be achieved when two coats are applied to a rough or weathered surface.

A stained surface should be refinished only when the colors fade and bare wood is beginning to show. A light steel-wooling or steel brushing with the grain and hosing with water to remove surface dirt and mildew is all that is needed to prepare the surface. Re-stain after the surfaces have thoroughly dried.

A number of penetrating pigmented stains finishes are on the market, or a satisfactory version can be prepared by home-mixing the Forest Products Laboratory natural finish.[3] This finish has a linseed oil vehicle; a preservative, pentachlorophenol, to protect the oil from mildew; and a water repellent, paraffin wax, to protect the wood from excessive penetration of water.

Clear Film Finishes

Clear finishes based on varnish, which form a coating or film on the surface, should not be used on wood exposed fully to the weather. These finishes are quite expensive and often begin to deteriorate within 1 year. Refinishing is a frequent, difficult, and time-consuming process.

Exterior Paints

Of all the finishes, paints provide the widest selection of color. When properly selected and applied, paint will provide the most protection to wood against weathering.

The durability of paint coatings on exterior wood, however, is affected by many variables, and much care is needed in the selection of the wood surface material, type of paint, and method of application to achieve success in painting. The original and maintenance costs are higher for a paint finish than for either the water-repellent-preservative treatment or penetrating-stain finish.

Paint performance is affected by such wood variables as species, density, structure, extractives, and defects such as knots and pitch pockets.

Best paint durability will be achieved on the select high grades of vertical-grain western redcedar, redwood, and low-density pines. Exterior-grade plywood which has been overlaid with medium-density resin-treated paper is another wood-base material on which paint will perform very well.

Follow these three simple steps when painting wood:

(1) Apply water-repellent preservative to all joints by brushing or spraying. Treat all lap and butt joints, ends and edges of lumber, and window sash and trim. Allow 2 warm days of drying before painting.

(2) Prime the treated wood surface with an oil-base paint free of zinc-oxide pigment. Do not use a porous low-luster oil paint as primer on wood surfaces. Apply sufficient primer so the grain of the wood cannot be seen. Open joints should be calked after priming.

(3) Apply two topcoats of high-quality oil, alkyd, or latex paint over the primer. The south side has the most severe exposure, so two topcoats are particularly important on that side of the house.

Effect of Impregnated Preservatives on Painting

Wood treated with the water-soluble preservatives in common use can be painted satisfactorily after it is redried. The coating may not last quite as long as it would have on untreated wood, but there is no vast difference. Certainly, a slight loss in durability is not enough to offer any practical objection to using treated wood where preservation against decay is necessary, protection against weathering desired, and appearance of painted wood important. Coal-tar creosote or other dark oily preservatives tend to stain through paint unless the treated wood has been exposed to the weather for many months before it is painted.

REPAINTING

(1) Repaint only when the old paint has worn thin and no longer protects the wood. Faded or dirty paint can often be freshened by washing. Where wood surfaces are exposed, spot prime with a zinc-free linseed oil primer before applying the finish coat. Too-frequent repainting produces an excessively thick film that is more sensitive to the weather and also is likely to crack abnormally across the grain of the paint. The grain of the paint is in the direction of the last brush strokes. Complete paint removal is the only cure for cross-grain cracking.

(2) Use the same brand and type of paint originally applied for the topcoat. A change is advisable only if a paint has given trouble. When repainting with latex paint, apply

---

[3] The composition, preparation, and application of the stain is described in "Forest Products Laboratory Natural Finish," USDA Forest Serv. Res. Note FPL–046, available from the Forest Products Laboratory, Forest Service, U.S. Department of Agriculture, Madison, Wis. It is also listed in Fed. Spec. TT–S–708a, "Stain, Oil; Semi-Transparent, Wood Exterior," available from the Superintendent of Documents, U.S. Government Printing Office, Washington, D.C. 20402.

a nonporous, oil-base primer overall before applying the latex paint.

(3) To avoid intercoat peeling, which indicates a weak bond between coats of paint, clean the old painted surface well and allow no more than 2 weeks between coats in two-coat repainting. Do not repaint sheltered areas, such as eaves and porch ceilings, every time the weathered body of the house is painted. In repainting sheltered areas, wash the old paint surface with trisodium phosphate or detergent solution to remove surface contaminants that will interfere with adhesion of the new coat of paint. Following washing, rinse sheltered areas with copious amounts of water and let dry thoroughly before repainting. When intercoat peeling does occur, complete paint removal is the only satisfactory procedure.

Blistering and Peeling

When too much water gets into wood, the paint may blister and peel. The moisture blisters normally appear first and peeling follows. But sometimes the paint peels without blistering. At other times the blisters go unnoticed. Moisture blisters usually contain water when they form, or soon afterward, and eventually dry out. Small blisters may disappear completely on drying; however, fairly large ones may leave a rough spot on the surface. If the blistering is severe, the paint may peel.

New, thin coatings are more likely to blister because of too much moisture under them than old, thick coatings. The older and thicker coatings are too rigid to stretch, as they must to blister, and so are more prone to cracking and peeling. Where either of these occurs the old paint must be completely burned off, and re-siding may be more economical.

House construction features that will minimize water damage of outside paint are: (a) Wide roof overhang, (b) wide flashing under shingles at roof edges, (c) effective vapor barriers, (d) adequate eave troughs and properly hung downspouts, and (e) adequate ventilation of the house. If these features are lacking in a house, persistent blistering and peeling may occur.

Discoloration by Color Extractives

Water-soluble color extractives occur naturally in western redcedar and redwood. It is to these substances that the heartwood of these two species owes its attractive color, good stability, and natural decay resistance. Discoloration occurs when the extractives are dissolved and leached from the wood by water. When the solution of extractives reaches the painted surface, the water evaporates, leaving the extractives as a reddish-brown stain. The water that gets behind the paint and causes moisture blisters also causes migration of extractives. The discoloration produced by water wetting the siding from the back side frequently forms a rundown or streaked pattern.

The emulsion paints and the so-called "breather" or low-luster oil paints are more porous than conventional oil paints. If these are used on new wood without a good oil primer, or if any paint is applied too thinly on new wood (a skimpy two-coat paint job, for example), rain or even heavy dew can penetrate the coating and reach the wood. When the water dries from the wood, the extractives are brought to the surface of the paint. Discoloration of paint by this process forms a diffused pattern.

On rough surfaces, such as shingles, machine-grooved shakes, and rough-sawn lumber siding, it is difficult to obtain an adequately thick coating on the high points. Therefore, extractive staining is more likely to occur on such surfaces by water penetrating through the coating. But the reddish-brown extractives will be less conspicuous if dark-colored paints are used.

Interior Finishes

Interior finishes for wood and dry-wall or plaster surfaces are usually intended to serve one or more of the following purposes:

(1) Make the surface easy to clean.
(2) Enhance the natural beauty of wood.
(3) Achieve a desired color decor.
(4) Impart wear resistance.

The type of finish depends largely upon type of area and the use to which the area will be put. The various interior areas and finish systems employed in each are summarized in table 6. Wood surfaces can be finished either with a clear finish or a paint. Plaster-base materials are painted.

Preparing Old Surfaces

The repainting of old surfaces depends on materials used previously and their condition. Following are preparations required for certain conditions:

Table 6.—*What interior finish to use—and where*[1]

Item	Interior latex	Flat oil paint	Semi-gloss paint	Floor (wood) seal[2]	Varnish[2]	Floor or deck enamel
Wood floors	—	—	—	X	X	X
Wood paneling and trim	—	X	X	X	X	—
Kitchen and bathroom walls (smooth surface with good scrubbability)	—	—	X	—	—	—
Dry-wall and plaster (rougher surface)	X	X	—	—	—	—

[1] Check the paint can for manufacturer's recommendations on primer or undercoat.
[2] Paste wax can be applied over floor seal with varnish base.

(1) Complete removal of old paint is required in the following cases, and a new covering material may be more practical:

    (a) Kalsomine over sand-textured plaster.

    (b) Kalsomine applied alternately with oil-base paint.

    (c) Noncompatible paints that have resulted in intercoat peeling.

    (d) Paints applied in kitchens or other areas over a grease film.

(2) All plaster cracks should be repaired with fiberglass tape and plaster patching.

(3) Old varnish should be cleaned with strong trisodium and then painted soon after drying. Heavily alligatored varnish must be removed before cleaning.

(4) Old radiators painted gold or aluminum should be coated with bronzing liquid before painting.

(5) Plastered chimneys may have creosote soaking through the plaster resulting from an accumulation in the chimney. This will continue to soak through, so the wall should be framed out around the chimney before adding a new covering material.

Wood Floors

Hardwood floors of oak, birch, beech, and maple are usually finished by applying two coats of wood seal, also called floor seal, with light sanding or steel wooling between coats. A final coat of paste wax is then applied and buffed. This finish is easily maintained by rewaxing. The final coat can also be a varnish instead of a sealer. The varnish finishes are used when a high gloss is desired.

When floors are to be painted, an undercoater is used, and then at least one topcoat of floor and deck enamel is applied.

Wood Paneling and Trim

Wood trim and paneling are most commonly finished with a clear wood sealer or a stain-sealer combination and then topcoated, after sanding, with at least one additional coat of sealer or varnish. The final coat of sealer or varnish can also be covered with a heavy coat of paste wax to produce a surface which is easily maintained by rewaxing. Good depth in a clear finish can be achieved by finishing first with one coat of high-gloss varnish followed with a final coat of semigloss varnish.

Wood trim of nonporous species such as pine can also be painted by first applying a coat of primer or undercoater, followed with a coat of latex, flat, or semigloss oil-base paint. Semigloss and gloss paints are more resistant to soiling and are more easily cleaned by washing than the flat oil and latex paints. Trim of wood species such as oak and mahogany, which are porous, requires filling before painting.

Kitchen and Bathroom Walls

Kitchen and bathroom walls which normally are plaster or dry-wall construction are finished best with a coat of undercoater and two coats of semigloss enamel. This type of finish wears well, is easy to clean, and is quite resistant to moisture.

Dry-Wall and Plaster

Plaster and dry-wall surfaces which account for the major portion of the interior area are finished with two coats of either flat oil or latex paint. An initial treatment with size or sealer will improve holdout (reduce penetration of succeeding coats) and thus reduce the quantity of paint required for good coverage.

SUMMARY

This handbook has presented major points necessary to inspect an older dwelling, plan improvements for it, and accomplish the rehabilitation. The procedures given should produce a dwelling with all the comforts and conveniences of a modern house.

Appraisal for rehabilitation.—A good foundation and a square frame are generally good indicators that a house is worth rehabilitating; however, repair and replacement requirements should still be weighed against the increased value of the property. The location of the dwelling and condition of surrounding properties will influence the final decision.

Planning and rehabilitation.—A good plan for improvements is essential to complete rehabilitation. Changes in lifestyle over the years usually dictate some changes in the layout of the rehabilitated dwelling. The layout should be planned to accommodate the three major family functional areas—relaxation, working, and privacy. Good traffic circulation patterns between and within functional areas is important for convenience and liveability. Additional living space is sometimes available in an attic, basement, or attached garage.

Many older dwellings have desirable qualities of appearance that should be retained. If changes in appearance are planned, the most important considerations are unity and simplicity. All additions should be in keeping with the existing character.

Reconditioning details.—Some of the actual work of rehabilitation can be done by the relatively unskilled homeowner; however, it is advisable to seek professional help for plumbing, electrical wiring, and heating system. Certain carpentry jobs involving major structural changes may also require professional assistance. If leveling of the floor system is required, that should be the first step. After that, make roof repairs and changes in windows or exterior doors. Any changes in plumbing, electrical wiring, and heating should be completed before interior finish work is started.

If the dwelling must be occupied while work is in progress, do the necessary items at once and plan the remainder in projects with a breather space between them. Living in a mess continually may make the project "go sour." A sensible approach will result in a house with new life that will satisfy needs for years to come.

GLOSSARY OF HOUSING TERMS

Attic ventilators.—In houses, screen openings provided to ventilate an attic space. They are located in the soffit area as inlet ventilators and in the gable end or along the ridge as outlet ventilators. They can also consist of power-driven fans used as an exhaust system. (See also *Louver.*)

Backfill.—The replacement of excavated earth into a trench around and against a basement foundation.

Base or baseboard.—A board placed against the wall around a room next to the floor to finish properly between floor and plaster.

Base molding.—Molding used to trim the upper edge of interior baseboard.

Base shoe.—Molding used next to the floor on interior baseboard. Sometimes called a carpet strip.

Batten.—Narrow strips of wood used to cover joints or as decorative vertical members over plywood or wide boards.

Beam.—A structural member transversely supporting a load.

Bearing partition.—A partition that supports any vertical load in addition to its own weight.

Bearing wall.—A wall that supports any vertical load in addition to its own weight.

Blind-nailing.—Nailing in such a way that the nailheads are not visible on the face of the work—usually at the tongue of matched boards.

Boston ridge.—A method of applying asphalt or wood shingles at the ridge or at the hips of a roof as a finish.

Brace.—An inclined piece of framing lumber applied to wall or floor to stiffen the structure. Often used on walls as temporary bracing until framing has been completed.

Brick veneer.—A facing of brick laid against and fastened to sheathing of a frame wall or tile wall construction.

Built-up roof.—A roofing composed of three to five layers of asphalt felt laminated with coal tar, pitch, or asphalt. The top is finished with crushed slag or gravel. Generally used on flat or low-pitched roofs.

Butt joint.—The junction where the ends of two timbers or other members meet in a square-cut joint.

Casement frames and sash.—Frames of wood or metal enclosing part or all of the sash, which may be opened by means of hinges affixed to the vertical edges.

Casing.—Molding of various widths and thicknesses used to trim door and window openings at the jambs.

Checking.—Fissures that appear with age in many exterior paint coatings, at first superficial, but which in time may penetrate entirely through the coating.

Collar beam.—Nominal 1- or 2-inch-thick members connecting opposite roof rafters. They serve to stiffen the roof structure.

Column.—In architecture: A perpendicular supporting member, circular or rectangular in section, usually consisting of a base, shaft, and capital. In engineering: A vertical structural compression member which supports loads acting in the direction of its longitudinal axis.

Combination doors or windows.—Combination doors or windows used over regular openings. They provide winter insulation and summer protection and often have self-storing or removable glass and screen inserts. This eliminates the need for handling a different unit each season.

Condensation.—In a building: Beads or drops of water (and frequently frost in extremely cold weather) that accumulate on the inside of the exterior covering of a building when warm, moisture-laden air from the interior reaches a point where the temperature no longer permits the air to sustain the moisture it holds. Use of louvers or attic ventilators will reduce moisture condensation in attics. A vapor barrier under the gypsum lath or dry wall on exposed walls will reduce condensation in them.

Construction dry-wall.—A type of construction in which the interior wall finish is applied in a dry condition, generally in the form of sheet materials or wood paneling, as contrasted to plaster.

Construction, frame.—A type of construction in which the structural parts are wood or depend upon a wood frame for support. In codes, if masonry veneer is applied to the exterior walls, the classification of this type of construction is usually unchanged.

Coped joint.—See *Scribing.*

Corner bead.—A strip of formed sheet metal, sometimes combined with a strip of metal lath, placed on corners before plastering to reinforce them. Also, a strip of wood finish three-quarters-round or angular placed over a plastered corner for protection.

Corner boards.—Used as trim for the external corners of a house or other frame structure against which the ends of the siding are finished.

Corner braces.—Diagonal braces at the corners of frame structure to stiffen and strengthen the wall.

Let-in brace.—Nominal 1–inch–thick boards applied into notched studs diagonally.

Cornice.—Overhang of a pitched roof at the eave line, usually consisting of a facia board, a soffit for a closed cornice, and appropriate moldings.

Cornice return.—That portion of the cornice that returns on the gable end of a house.

Counterflashing.—A flashing usually used on chimneys at the roof line to cover shingle flashing and to prevent moisture entry.

Cove molding.—A molding with a concave face used as trim or to finish interior corners.

Crawl space.—A shallow space below the living quarters of a basementless house, normally enclosed by the foundation wall.

Cripple stud.—A stud that does not extend full height.

d.—See *Penny.*

Dado.—A rectangular groove across the width of a board or plank. In interior decoration, a special type of wall treatment.

Decay.—Disintegration of wood or other substance through the action of fungi.

Deck paint.—An enamel with a high degree of resistance to mechanical wear, designed for use on such surfaces as porch floors.

Density.—The mass of substance in a unit volume. When expressed in the metric system, it is numerically equal to the specific gravity of the same substance.

Dewpoint.—Temperature at which a vapor begins to deposit as a liquid. Applies especially to water in the atmosphere.

Dimension.—See *Lumber dimension.*

Direct nailing.—To nail perpendicular to the initial surface or to the junction of the pieces joined. Also termed *face nailing.*

Door jamb, interior.—The surrounding case into which and out of which a door closes and opens. It consists of two upright pieces, called side jambs, and a horizontal head jamb.

Dormer.—An opening in a sloping roof, the framing of which projects out to form a vertical wall suitable for windows or other openings.

Downspout.—A pipe, usually of metal, for carrying rainwater from roof gutters.

Dressed and matched (tongued and grooved).—Boards or planks machined in such a manner that there is a groove on one edge and a corresponding tongue on the other.

Drip.—(a) A member of a cornice or other horizontal exterior-finish course that has a projection beyond the other parts for throwing off water. (b) A groove in the underside of a sill or drip cap to cause water to drop off on the outer edge instead of drawing back and running down the face of the building.

Drip cap.—A molding placed on the exterior top side of a door or window frame to cause water to drip beyond the outside of the frame.

Dry-wall.—Interior covering material, such as gypsum board or plywood, which is applied in large sheets or panels.

Ducts.—In a house, usually round or rectangular metal pipes for distributing warm air from the heating plant to rooms, or air from a conditioning device or as cold air returns. Ducts are also made of asbestos and composition materials.

Eaves.—The margin or lower part of a roof projecting over the wall.

Facia or fascia.—A flat board, band, or face, used sometimes by itself but usually in combination with moldings, often located at the outer face of the cornice.

Filler (wood).—A heavily pigmented preparation used for filling and leveling off the pores in open-pored woods.

Fire stop.—A solid, tight closure of a concealed space, placed to prevent the spread of fire and smoke through such a space. In a frame wall, this will usually consist of 2 by 4 cross blocking between studs.

Fishplate.—A wood or plywood piece used to fasten the ends of two members together at a butt joint with nails or bolts. Sometimes used at the junction of opposite rafters near the ridge line.

Flashing.—Sheet metal or other material used in roof and wall construction to protect a building from water seepage.

Flat paint.—An interior paint that contains a high proportion of pigment and dries to a flat or lusterless finish.

Flue.—The space or passage in a chimney through which smoke, gas, or fumes ascend. Each passage is called a flue, which together with any others and the surrounding masonry make up the chimney.

Flue lining.—Fire clay or terra-cotta pipe, round or square, usually made in all ordinary flue sizes and in 2-foot lengths, used for the inner lining of chimneys with the brick or masonry work around the outside. Flue lining in chimney runs from about a foot below the flue connection to the top of the chimney.

Fly rafters.—End rafters of the gable overhang supported by roof sheathing and lookouts.

Footing.—A masonry section, usually concrete, in a rectangular form wider than the bottom of the foundation wall or pier it supports.

Foundation.—The supporting portion of a structure below the first-floor construction, or below grade, including the footings.

Framing, balloon.—A system of framing a building in which all vertical structural elements of the bearing walls and partitions consist of single pieces extending from the top of the foundation sill plate to the roofplate and to which all floor joists are fastened.

Framing, platform.—A system of framing a building in which floor joists of each story rest on top plates of the story below or on the foundation sill for the first story, and the bearing walls and partitions rest on the subfloor of each story.

Frieze.—In house construction, a horizontal member connecting the top of the siding with the soffit of the cornice.

Frostline.—The depth of frost penetration in soil. This depth varies in different parts of the country. Footings should be placed below this depth to prevent movement.

Fungi, wood.—Microscopic plants that live in damp wood and cause mold, stain, and decay.

Fungicide.—A chemical that is poisonous to fungi.

Furring.—Strips of wood or metal applied to a wall or other surface to even it and normally to serve as a fastening base for finish material.

Gable.—In house construction, the portion of the roof above the eave line of a double-sloped roof.

Gable end.—An end wall having a gable.

Gloss enamel.—A finishing material made of varnish and sufficient pigments to provide opacity and color, but little or no pigment of low opacity. Such an enamel forms a hard coating with maximum smoothness of surface and a high degree of gloss.

Gloss (paint or enamel). A paint or enamel that contains a relatively low proportion of pigment and dries to a sheen or luster.

Girder.—A large or principal beam of wood or steel used

to support concentrated loads at isolated points along its length.

Grain.—The direction, size arrangement, appearance, or quality of the fibers in wood.

Grain, edge (vertical).—Edge-grain lumber has been sawed parallel to the pith of the log and approximately at right angles to the growth rings; i.e., the rings form an angle of 45° or more with the surface of the piece.

Grain, flat.—Flat-grain lumber has been sawed parallel to the pitch of the log and approximately tangent to the growth rings, i.e., the rings form an angle of less than 45° with the surface of the piece.

Grain, quartersawn.—Another term for edge grain.

Grounds.—Guides used around openings and at the floorline to strike off plaster. They can consist of narrow strips of wood or of wide subjambs at interior doorways. They provide a level plaster line for installation of casing and other trim.

Grout.—Mortar made of such consistency (by adding water) that it will just flow into the joints and cavities of the masonry work and fill them solid.

Gusset.—A flatwood, plywood, or similar type member used to provide a connection at intersection of wood members. Most commonly used at joints of wood trusses. They are fastened by nails, screws, bolts, or adhesives.

Gutter or eave trough.—A shallow channel or conduit of metal or wood set below and along the eaves of a house to catch and carry off rainwater from the roof.

Gypsum plaster.—Gypsum formulated to be used with the addition of sand and water for base-coat plaster.

Header.—(a) A beam placed perpendicular to joists and to which joists are nailed in framing for chimney, stairway, or other opening. (b) A wood lintel.

Heartwood.—The wood extending from the pith to the sapwood, the cells of which no longer participate in the life processes of the tree.

Hip.—The external angle formed by the meeting of two sloping sides of a roof.

Hip roof.—A roof that rises by inclined planes from all four sides of a building.

Humidifier.—A device designed to increase the humidity within a room or a house by means of the discharge of water vapor. They may consist of individual room-size units or larger units attached to the heating plant to condition the entire house.

Insulation board, rigid.—A structural building board made of coarse wood or cane fiber in $1/2$- or $25/32$-inch thicknesses. It can be obtained in various size sheets, in various densities, and with several treatments.

Insulation, thermal.—Any material high in resistance to heat transmission that, when placed in the walls, ceiling, or floors of a structure, will reduce the rate of heat flow.

Interior finish.—Material used to cover the interior framed areas, or materials of walls and ceilings.

Jack post.—A hollow metal post with a jack screw in one end so it can be adjusted to the desired height.

Jack rafter.—A rafter that spans the distance from the wallplate to a hip, or from a valley to a ridge.

Jamb.—The side and head lining of a doorway, window, or other opening.

Joint.—The space between the adjacent surfaces of two members or components joined and held together by nails, glue, cement, mortar, or other means.

Joint cement.—A powder that is usually mixed with water and used for joint treatment in gypsum-wallboard finish. Often called "spackle."

Joist.—One of a series of parallel beams, usually 2 inches in thickness, used to support floor and ceiling loads, and supported in turn by larger beams, girders, or bearing walls.

Knot.—In lumber, the portion of a branch or limb of a tree that appears on the edge or face of the piece.

Landing.—A platform between flights of stairs or at the termination of a flight of stairs.

Lath.—A building material of wood, metal, gypsum, or insulating board that is fastened to the frame of a building to act as a plaster base.

Ledger strip.—A strip of lumber nailed along the bottom of the side of a girder on which joists rest.

Lintel.—A horizontal structural member that supports the load over an opening such as a door or window.

Lookout.—A short wood bracket or cantilever to support an overhang portion of a roof or the like, usually concealed from view.

Louver.—An opening with a series of horizontal slats so arranged as to permit ventilation but to exclude rain, sunlight, or vision. See also *Attic ventilators.*

Lumber.—Lumber is the product of the sawmill and planing mill not further manufactured other than by sawing, resawing, and passing lengthwise through a standard planing machine, crosscutting to length, and matching.

Lumber, boards.—Yard lumber less than 2 inches thick and 2 or more inches wide.

Lumber, dimension.—Yard lumber from 2 inches to, but not including, 5 inches thick and 2 or more inches wide. Includes joists, rafters, studs, plank, and small timbers.

Lumber, dressed size.—The dimension of lumber after shrinking from green dimension and after machining to size or pattern.

Lumber, matched.—Lumber that is dressed and shaped on one edge in a grooved pattern and on the other in a tongued pattern.

Lumber, shiplap.—Lumber that is edge-dressed to make a close rabbeted or lapped joint.

Lumber, timbers.—Yard lumber 5 or more inches in least dimension. Includes beams, stringers, posts, caps, sills, girders, and purlins.

Lumber, yard.—Lumber of those grades, sizes, and patterns which are generally intended for ordinary construction, such as framework and rough coverage of houses.

Mantel.—The shelf above a fireplace. Also used in referring to the decorative trim around a fireplace opening.

Masonry.—Stone, brick, concrete, hollow-tile, concrete-block, gypsum-block, or other similar building units or materials or a combination of the same, bonded together with mortar to form a wall, pier, buttress, or similar mass.

Mastic.—A pasty material used as a cement (as for setting tile) or a protective coating (as for thermal insulation or waterproofing).

Metal lath.—Sheets of metal that are slit and drawn out to form openings. Used as a plaster base for walls and ceilings and as reinforcing over other forms of plaster base.

Millwork.—Generally all building materials made of finished wood and manufactured in millwork plants and planing mills are included under the term "millwork." It includes such items as inside and outside doors, window and door frames, blinds, porchwork, mantels, panelwork, stairways, moldings, and interior trim. It normally does not include flooring, ceiling, or siding.

Miter joint.—The joint of two pieces at an angle that bisects the joining angle. For example, the miter joint at the side and head casing as a door opening is made at a 45° angle.

Moisture content of wood.—Weight of the water contained in the wood, usually expressed as a percentage of the weight of the ovendry wood.

Molding.—A wood strip having a curved or projecting surface used for decorative purposes.

Mullion.—A vertical bar or divider in the frame between windows, doors, or other openings.

Muntin.—A small member which divides the glass or openings of sash or doors.

Natural finish.—A transparent finish which does not seriously alter the original color or grain of the natural wood. Natural finishes are usually provided by sealers, oils, varnishes, water-repellent preservatives, and other similar materials.

Nonbearing wall.—A wall supporting no load other than its own weight.

Nosing.—The projecting edge of a molding or drip. Usually applied to the projecting molding on the edge of a stair tread.

O. C., on center.—The measurement of spacing for studs, rafters, joists, and the like in a building from the center of one member to the center of the next.

Outrigger.—An extension of a rafter beyond the wall line. Usually a smaller member nailed to a larger rafter to form a cornice or roof overhang.

Paint.—A combination of pigments with suitable thinners or oils to provide decorative and protective coatings.

Panel.—In house construction, a thin flat piece of wood, plywood, or similar material, framed by stiles and rails as in a door or fitted into grooves of thicker material with molded edges for decorative wall treatment.

Paper, building.—A general term for papers, felts, and similar sheet materials used in buildings without reference to their properties or uses.

Paper, sheathing.—A building material, generally paper or felt, used in wall and roof construction as a protection against the passage of air and sometimes moisture.

Parting stop or strip.—A small wood piece used in the side and head jambs of double-hung windows to separate upper and lower sash.

Partition.—A wall that subdivides spaces within any story of a building.

Penny.—As applied to nails, it originally indicated the price per hundred. The term now serves as a measure of nail length and is abbreviated by the letter *d*.

Perm.—A measure of water vapor movement through a material (grains per square foot per hour per inch of mercury difference in vapor pressure).

Pier.—A column of masonry, usually rectangular in horizontal cross section, used to support other structural members.

Pigment.—A powdered solid in suitable degree of subdivision for use in paint or enamel.

Pitch.—The incline slope of a roof or the ratio of the total rise to the total width of a house, i.e., an 8-foot rise and 24-foot width is a one-third pitch roof. Roof slope is expressed in the inches of rise per foot of run.

Pith.—The small, soft core at the original center of a tree around which wood formation takes place.

Plaster grounds.—Strips of wood used as guides or strike-off edges around window and door openings and at base of walls.

Plate.—Sill plate: A horizontal member anchored to a masonry wall. Sole plate: Bottom horizontal member of a frame wall. Top plate: Top horizontal member of a frame wall supporting ceiling joists; rafters, or other members.

Plough.—To cut a lengthwise groove in a board or plank.

Plumb.—Exactly perpendicular; vertical.

Ply.—A term to denote the number of thicknesses or layers of roofing felt, veneer in plywood, or layers in built-up materials, in any finished piece of such material.

Plywood.—A piece of wood made of three or more layers of veneer joined with glue, and usually laid with the grain of adjoining plies at right angles. Almost always an odd number of plies are used to provide balanced construction.

Preservative.—Any substance that, for a reasonable length of time, will prevent the action of wood-destroying fungi, borers of various kinds, and similar destructive agents when the wood has been properly coated or impregnated with it.

Primer.—The first coat of paint in a paint job that consists of two or more coats; also the paint used for such a first coat.

Putty.—A type of cement usually made of whiting and boiled linseed oil, beaten or kneaded to the consistency of dough, and used in sealing glass in sash, filling small holes and crevices in wood, and for similar purposes.

Quarter round.—A small molding that has the cross section of a quarter circle.

Rabbet.—A rectangular longitudinal groove cut in the corner edge of a board or plank.

Radiant heating.—A method of heating, usually consisting of a forced hot water system with pipes placed in the floor, wall, or ceiling; or with electrically heated panels.

Rafter.—One of a series of structural members of a roof designed to support roof loads. The rafters of a flat roof are sometimes called roof joists.

Rafter, hip.—A rafter that forms the intersection of an external roof angle.

Rafter, valley.—A rafter that forms the intersection of an internal roof angle. The valley rafter is normally made of double 2–inch–thick members.

Rail.—Cross members of panel doors or of a sash. Also the upper and lower members of a balustrade or staircase extending from one vertical support, such as a post, to another.

Rake.—Trim members that run parallel to the roof slope and form the finish between the wall and a gable roof extension.

Reflective insulation.—Sheet material with one or both surfaces of comparatively low heat emissivity, such as aluminium foil. When used in building construction the surfaces face air spaces, reducing the radiation across the air space.

Reinforcing.—Steel rods or metal fabric placed in concrete slabs, beams, or columns to increase their strength.

Relative humidity.—The amount of water vapor in the atmosphere, expressed as a percentage of the maximum quantity that could be present at a given temperature. (The actual amount of water vapor that can be held in space increases with the temperature.)

Ribbon (Girt).—Normally a 1– by 4–inch board let into the studs horizontally to support ceiling or second-floor joists.

Ridge.—The horizontal line at the junction of the top edges of two sloping roof surfaces.

Ridge board.—The board placed on edge at the ridge of the roof into which the upper ends of the rafters are fastened.

Rise.—In stairs, the vertical height of a step or flight of stairs.

Riser.—Each of the vertical boards closing the spaces between the treads of stairways.

Roll roofing.—Roofing material, composed of fiber and saturated with asphalt, that is supplied in 36–inch wide rolls with 108 square feet of material. Weights are generally 45 to 90 pounds per roll.

Roof sheathing.—The boards or sheet material fastened to the roof rafters on which the shingle or other roof covering is laid.

Rout.—The removal of material, by cutting, milling or gouging, to form a groove.

Run.—In stairs, the net width of a step or the horizontal distance covered by a flight of stairs.

Saddle.—Two sloping surfaces meeting in a horizontal ridge, used between the back side of a chimney, or other vertical surface, and a sloping roof.

Sapwood.—The outer zone of wood, next to the bark. In the living tree it contains some living cells (the heartwood contains none), as well as dead and dying cells. In most species, it is lighter colored than the heartwood. In all species, it is lacking in decay resistance.

Sash.—A single light frame containing one or more lights of glass.

Saturated felt.—A felt which is impregnated with tar or asphalt.

Scratch coat.—The first coat of plaster, which is scratched to form a bond for the second coat.

Screed.—A small strip of wood, usually the thickness of the plaster coat, used as a guide for plastering.

Scribing.—Fitting woodwork to an irregular surface. In moldings, cutting the end of one piece to fit the molded face of the other at an interior angle to replace a miter joint.

Sealer.—A finishing material, either clear or pigmented, that is usually applied directly over uncoated wood for the purpose of sealing the surface.

Semigloss paint or enamel.—A paint or enamel made with a slight insufficiency of nonvolatile vehicle so that its coating, when dry, has some luster but is not very glossy.

Shake.—A thick handsplit shingle, resawed to form two shakes, usually edge-grained.

Sheathing.—The structural covering, usually wood boards or plywood, used over studs or rafters of a structure. Structural building board is normally used only as wall sheathing.

Sheathing paper.—See *Paper, sheathing.*

Sheet metal work.—All components of a house employing sheet metal, such as flashing, gutters, and downspouts.

Shellac.—A transparent coating made by dissolving *lac*, a resinous secretion of the lac bug (a scale insect that thrives in tropical countries, especially India), in alcohol.

Shingles.—Roof covering of asphalt, asbestos, wood, tile, slate, or other material cut to stock lengths, width, and thicknesses.

Shingles, siding.—Various kinds of shingles, such as wood shingles or shakes and nonwood shingles, that are used over sheathing for exterior sidewall covering of a structure.

Shiplap.—See *Lumber, shiplap.*

Shutter.—Usually lightweight louvered or flush wood or nonwood frames in the form of doors located at each side of a window. Some are made to close over the window for protection; others are fastened to the wall as a decorative device.

Siding.—The finish covering of the outside wall of a frame building, whether made of horizontal weatherboards, vertical boards with battens, shingles, or other material.

Siding, bevel (lap siding).—Wedge-shaped boards used as horizontal siding in a lapped pattern. This siding varies in butt thickness from $1/2$ to $3/4$ inch and in widths up to 12 inches. Normally used over some type of sheathing.

Siding, Dolly Varden.—Beveled wood siding which is rabbeted on the bottom edge.

Siding, drop.—Usually ³/₄ inch thick and 6 and 8 inches wide with tongued-and-grooved or shiplap edges. Often used as siding without sheathing in secondary buildings.

Sill.—The lowest member of the frame of a structure, resting on the foundation and supporting the floor joists or the uprights of the wall. The member forming the lower side of an opening, as a door sill, window sill, etc.

Sleeper.—Usually, a wood member embedded in concrete, as in a floor, that serves to support and to fasten subfloor or flooring.

Soffit.—Usually the underside of an overhanging cornice.

Soil cover (ground cover).—A light covering of plastic film, roll roofing, or similar material used over the soil in crawl spaces of buildings to minimize moisture permeation of the area.

Soil stack.—A general term for the vertical main of a system of soil, waste, or vent piping.

Sole or sole plate.—See *Plate.*

Solid bridging.—A solid member placed between adjacent floor joists near the center of the span to prevent joists from twisting.

Span.—The distance between structural supports such as walls, columns, piers, beams, girders, and trusses.

Splash block.—A small masonry block laid with the top close to the ground surface to receive roof drainage from downspouts and to carry it away from the building.

Square.—A unit of measure—100 square feet—usually applied to roofing material. Sidewall coverings are sometimes packed to cover 100 square feet and are sold on that basis.

Stain, shingle.—A form of oil paint, very thin in consistency, intended for coloring wood with rough surfaces, such as shingles, without forming a coating of significant thickness or gloss.

Stair carriage.—Supporting member for stair treads. Usually a 2–inch plank notched to receive the treads; sometimes called a "rough horse."

Stair landing.—See *Landing.*

Stair rise.—See *Rise.*

Stile.—An upright framing member in a panel door.

Stool.—A flat molding fitted over the window sill between jambs and contacting the bottom rail of the lower sash.

Storm sash or storm window.—An extra window usually placed on the outside of an existing one as additional protection against cold weather.

Story.—That part of a building between any floor and the floor or roof next above.

Strike plate.—A metal plate mortised into or fastened to the face of a door-frame side jamb to receive the latch or bolt when the door is closed.

Strip flooring.—Wood flooring consisting of narrow, matched strips.

String, stringer.—A timber or other support for cross members in floors or ceilings. In stairs, the support on which the stair treads rest; also stringboard.

Stucco.—Most commonly refers to an outside plaster made with Portland cement as its base.

Stud.—One of a series of slender wood or metal vertical structural members placed as supporting elements in walls and partitions. (Plural: Studs or studding.)

Subfloor.—Boards or plywood laid on joists over which a finish floor is to be laid.

Suspended ceiling.—A ceiling system supported by hanging it from the overhead structural framing.

Termites.—Insects that superficially resemble ants in size, general appearance, and habit of living in colonies; hence, they are frequently called "white ants." Subterranean termites establish themselves in buildings not by being carried in with lumber, but by entering from ground nests after the building has been constructed. If unmolested, they eat out the woodwork, leaving a shell of sound wood to conceal their activities, and damage may proceed so far as to cause collapse of parts of a structure before discovery. There are about 56 species of termites known in the United States; but the two major ones, classified by the manner in which they attack wood, are ground-inhabiting or subterranean termites (the most common) and dry-wood termites, which are found almost exclusively along the extreme southern border and the Gulf of Mexico in the United States.

Threshold.—A strip of wood or metal with beveled edges used over the finish floor and the sill of exterior doors.

Toenailing.—To drive a nail at a slant with the initial surface in order to permit it to penetrate into a second member.

Tongued and grooved.—See *Dressed and matched.*

Tread.—The horizontal board in a stairway on which the foot is placed.

Trim.—The finish materials in a building, such as moldings, applied around openings (window trim, door trim) or at the floor and ceiling of rooms (baseboard, cornice, and other moldings).

Trimmer.—A beam or joist to which a header is nailed in framing for a chimney, stairway, or other opening.

Truss.—A frame or jointed structure designed to act as a beam of long span, while each member is usually subjected to longitudinal stress only, either tension or compression.

Turpentine.—A volatile oil used as a thinner in paints and as a solvent in varnishes. Chemically, it is a mixture of terpenes.

Undercoat.—A coating applied prior to the finishing or top coats of a paint job. It may be the first of two or the second of three coats. In some usage of the word it may become synonymous with priming coat.

Underlayment.—A material placed under finish coverings, such as flooring, or shingles, to provide a smooth, even surface for applying the finish.

Valley.—The internal angle formed by the junction of two sloping sides of a roof.

Vapor barrier.—Material used to retard the movement of water vapor into walls and prevent condensation in them. Usually considered as having a perm value of less than 1.0. Applied separately over the warm side of exposed walls or as a part of batt or blanket insulation.

Varnish.—A thickened preparation of drying oil or drying oil and resin suitable for spreading on surfaces to form continuous, transparent coatings, or for mixing with pigments to make enamels.

Vehicle.—The liquid portion of a finishing material; it consists of the binder (nonvolatile) and volatile thinners.

Veneer.—Thin sheets of wood made by rotary cutting or slicing of a log.

Vent.—A pipe or duct which allows flow of air as an inlet or outlet.

Water-repellent preservative.—A liquid designed to penetrate into wood and impart water repellency and a moderate preservative protection. It is used for millwork, such as sash and frames, and is usually applied by dipping.

Weatherstrip.—Narrow or jamb-width sections of thin metal or other material to prevent infiltration of air and moisture around windows and doors, Compression weather stripping prevent air infiltration, provides tension, and acts a counterbalance.

INDEX

Page

Additions for existing houses:
Additional rooms ---------------------- 21, 73, 79
Bathroom ---------------------------- 23
Partitions --------------------------- 59
Roof overhang ------------------------ 25
Windows ----------------------------- 47
Appearance, wood-frame structures:
Appraisal for rehabilitation -------------- 13
Changes contemplated --------------- 13, 25
Appraisal for rehabilitation, summary ---------- 83
Asphalt shingles:
Application ------------------------ 43, 46
For roofs --------------------------- 6, 57
Nailing ----------------------------- 46
Asphalt tile -------------------------- 35
Attic:
Ceilings ----------------------------- 75
Chimney ---------------------------- 75
Expansion ------------------------ 19, 73
Finishing ---------------------------- 73
Gable dormers ------------------------ 73
Insulation ------------------------ 19, 55
Knee walls --------------------------- 74
Layout ------------------------------ 19
Shed dormer -------------------------- 74
Ventilation ---------------------- 57, 58, 84
Baseboard:
Installation --------------------------- 67
Nailing ------------------------------ 67
Types ------------------------------- 66
Basements:
Ceilings ----------------------------- 78
Damp ----------------------------- 3, 20, 75
Expansion ---------------------------- 20
Finishing ---------------------------- 75
Floors ------------------------------ 75
Insulation on walls ---------------- 20, 75, 78
Posts ------------------------------- 30
Protection from termites ---------------- 30
Walls ------------------------------- 77
Bathroom, addition to wood-frame structure:
Fixtures ----------------------------- 24
Framing bathtub ----------------------- 70
Interior finishes ----------------------- 83
Minimum size ------------------------- 24
Batt-type insulation ------------------ 54, 55
Bevel siding -------------------------- 37
Blanket insulation with vapor barrier -------- 54, 56
Blistering and peeling of paint ------------- 82
Boston ridge in roofs ------------------ 46, 84
Built-up roof coverings ----------------- 46, 84
Built-up roofing, appraisal for rehabilitation ------ 6
Carpenter ants ------------------------ 9
Carpet installation ------------------- 34, 75
Casement window ---------------------- 5, 47
Casing:
Installation ------------------------ 53, 66
Nailing ---------------------------- 53, 66

Page

Patterns ---------------------------- 53, 66
Sizes ------------------------------ 53, 66
Cathedral ceilings ------------------ 10, 58, 75
Ceiling insulation:
Batt -------------------------------- 54
Blanket ----------------------------- 54
Loose-fill type ----------------------- 54
Thickness recommended ---------------- 54
Ceiling moldings ---------------------- 67
Ceiling tile:
Fastening ---------------------------- 65
Installation --------------------------- 65
Nailing ------------------------------ 65
Ceilings:
Attic ------------------------------- 75
Basement --------------------------- 78
Cathedral ------------------------- 58, 75
Finished with gypsum board and other sheet materials ------ 64
Finished with tile --------------------- 65
Garage ------------------------------ 79
Insulation ------------------------ 10, 54
Moldings ---------------------------- 67
Patching involved when removing partitions ------- 18, 59
Suspended ceiling ---------------- 64, 65, 78
Chimneys and fireplaces:
Flue linings -------------------------- 71
Masonry and concrete ---------------- 3, 71
Replacing defective -------------------- 71
Circulation --------------------------- 12
Clapboard siding ---------------------- 37
Clear film finishes -------------------- 81
Closets:
Altering existing closets ---------------- 68
Layout ------------------------------ 18
New closets -------------------------- 69
Concrete walls ------------------------- 3
Continuous membrane vapor barrier ---------- 56
Control of moisture:
Insulation ---------------------------- 54
Vapor barriers ----------------------- 55
Ventilation --------------------------- 57
Corridor-type kitchen ------------------- 22
Cracks in concrete foundation --------------- 30
Crawl space:
Insulated floor --------------------- 10, 55
Protection from termites ---------------- 26
Soil cover ---------------------------- 56
Ventilation ------------------------ 56, 58
Crumbling mortar in foundations ------------ 30
Cutting floor joists for utilities ------------- 69
Damp basements --------------------- 3, 20
Decay and insects:
Foundations and floors ------------------ 8
Porches ------------------------------ 8
Recognizing decay --------------------- 7
Roof system --------------------------- 8
Siding and exterior trim ----------------- 8
Windows and doors --------------------- 8
Decorative moldings -------------------- 67

	Page
Developing rehabilitation plan, summary	16
Discoloration by color extractives	82
Door casing:	
Nailing	66
Styles	66
Thicknesses	66
Doors, wood-frame houses:	
Appraisal for rehabilitation	5
Decay in	8
Exterior doors	49, 51
Framing	49, 52
Interior doors	52, 54
Installation	49, 52
Nailing	49
Placement in remodeled kitchens	22
Standard door height	49, 54
Sticking doors	49
Weatherstripping	5, 51, 54
Double-course shingle siding	39
Double-hung window	47
Draining system	11
Drip cap, in siding installation	35, 85
Drywall:	
Interior finishes	58, 83
Thicknesses	58, 62
Types	58
Electric panel heating	12
Electrical heating	12
Electrical system, appraisal for rehabilitation	12
Expansion in wood-frame structures:	
Addition	21
Attic	19
Basement	20
Bathroom	24
Garage	21
Exterior doors:	
Hinges	49, 51
Installation	49
Nailing	49
Standard height	49
Styles	49
Types	49
Weatherstripping	51
Exterior paints:	
Application	81
Priming	81
Repainting	81
Species recommended	81
Exterior structural wood-frame:	
Doors	5
Finishes	5, 6
Porches	5
Roof	6
Siding and trim	4
Windows	5
Exterior-type plywood	26
Fiberboard, interior finish	60, 64
Final evaluation for rehabilitating structures:	
Cautions	14
Cost	14
Location	14
Reasons for rejection	14
Sentimental value	14
Finishes, wood-frame houses:	
See Painting and finishing.	
Finishing basements:	
Ceilings	78
Floors	75, 76
Walls	77
Finishing garages:	
Additions	79

	Page
Ceilings	79
Floors	78
Walls	79
Flashing, roof	6, 44, 73, 85
Floor coverings:	
Laying floor	33
Types	34
Floor framing:	
Appraisal for rehabilitation	6
Elimination of squeaks	31, 32
Leveling of floor	31
Replacement of framing members	31
Sagging floor joists	31
Strip flooring	32, 33
Supports	4, 31
Undersized floor joists	4, 31
Floor furnace	11
Fooring:	
Asphalt tile	35
Carpeting	34, 75
Linoleum	35
Particleboard tile	34
Resilient tile, appraisal for rehabilitation	6
Seamless flooring	34
Sheet vinyl	34
Strip flooring	33
Wood-base tile	34
Wood block flooring	34
Wood floors, appraisal for rehabilitation	6
Floor insulation:	
Application	55
Batt-type	55
Blanket	55
Floor supports, appraisal for rehabilitation	4
Floors:	
Basement	55
Garage	78
Insulation	55
Interior finishes	83
Patching when removing partitions	59
Porches	72
Forest Products Laboratory natural finish	81
Framing:	
Bathtub	70
Doors	49, 52
Foundations:	
Appraisal for rehabilitation	1
Basement posts	30
Chimneys and fireplaces	3
Concrete walls	3
Cracks in	3, 30
Crumbling mortar	3, 30
Damp basements	3
Decay in	8
Masonry and concrete	3
Masonry veneers	3
Uneven settlement	30
Walls and piers	3
Wood piers	3
Framing materials, moisture content recommended	26
Framing, roof:	
Appraisal for rehabilitation	4
Built-up	46
Flashing	44, 46
In partitions being added	41, 42
Overhang	42
Gable dormer:	
Flashing	74
Framing	73
Roof	73
Siding	74

	Page
Ventilation	58
Garage:	
Expansion	21
Finishing	21
Floors	21, 78
Insulating	21, 79
Roof	78
Glossary of housing terms	84
Gravity steam heat	11
Gravity warm air furnaces	11
Gypsum board, interior finish:	
Applied to ceiling joists	64
Cost	63
Finishing	63
Labor involved	63
Nailing	63, 64
Preparing for painting	63
Sizes	63
Hardboard siding	36, 37
Hardwood flooring	33
Heating, structural wood-frame:	
Appraisal for rehabilitation	11
Electric panel	12
Electrical heating	12
Floor furnace	11
Gravity steam heat	11
Gravity warm air	11
Radiant	12
Hollow-core doors	49, 54
Horizontal wood siding:	
Application	37
Bevel	37
Clapboard siding	37
Nailing	37
Impregnated preservatives, effect on painting	81
Inadequate nailing, cause of squeaking	32
Insect problems:	
Carpenter ants	9
Powder-post beetles	9
Termites	9
Insulation:	
Blanket insulation with vapor barrier	56
Causes of heat loss	54
Ceiling	54
Floor	55
On masonry walls	55, 78
Wall	54
Insulation and control of moisture:	
Appraisal for rehabilitation	10
Insulation	19, 54
Vapor barriers	19, 55
Ventilation	19
Intercoat paint peeling, avoiding	82
Interior covering, appraisal for rehabilitation	6
Interior doors:	
Framing	52
Installation	52
Patterns	54
Standard door height	49
Types	54
Widths	54
Interior finish:	
Ceiling tile	65
Gypsum board	58, 63
Plywood and hardboard	58, 63
Wood and fiberboard paneling	58, 64
Interior finish woodwork, moisture content recommended	26
Interior finishes:	
Application	83
Purpose	82
Wood floors	83

	Page
Interior finishes for:	
Dry-wall and plaster	60, 82
Kitchen and bathroom walls	82
Preparing old surfaces	82
Wood floors	82
Wood paneling and trim	82
Interior structural wood-frame:	
Flooring	6
Interior covering	6
Painted surfaces	7
Trim, cabinets and doors	7
Walls and ceilings	6
Interior trim:	
Baseboard	66
Casing	66
Ceiling moldings	67
Decorative moldings	67
Interior wall finish	60
Kitchen cabinets:	
New cabinets	68
Repair of existing cabinets	22, 67
Kitchens:	
Interior finishing	83
Remodeling	22
Knee walls	74
L-type kitchen	22
Layout, structural wood-frame:	
Appearance	13
Private area	12
Relaxation area	13
Work area	12
Layout, wood-frame structures:	
Attic	19
Basement	20
Changing partitions	17
Closets	18
Expansion	21
General	12, 16
Porches	19
Traffic circulation	12, 16, 17
Window placement	18
Zoned living	16
Leveling uneven floors	31
Linoleum:	
Sizes	35
Underlayment required	34
Lock sets, doors	51, 53
Masonry veneer:	
Foundations	1
Siding	41
Mechanical systems, structural wood-frame	10
Moisture content:	
Framing material	26
Interior finish woodwork	26
Moldings, ceiling	67
Nailing:	
Door casing	49, 53
Doors	49
Floor installation	33
Gypsum board interior finish	63, 64
Partitions being added	60
Roof sheathing	42, 45, 46
Shingle applications	42, 45
Siding installation	34, 37, 38, 40
Wood and fiberboard paneling for interior finish	64
Nonsubterranean termites	9
Overhang, roof	6, 25, 42
Paint discoloration by color extractives	82
Painted surfaces:	
Appraisal for rehabilitation	6
Interior	82

Page

Painting and finishing:
Appraisal for rehabilitation _____ 6
Blistering and peeling _____ 82
Clear film finishes _____ 81
Discoloration by color extractives _____ 82
Dry-wall and plaster _____ 83
Effect of impregnated preservatives on painting _____ 81
Exterior paint _____ 81
FPL natural finish _____ 81
Interior finishes _____ 82
Penetrating pigmented stain finishes _____ 80
Repainting _____ 81, 83
Types of exterior finishes _____ 81
Water-repellent preservative finishes _____ 80
Wood properties and finish durability _____ 80
Panel siding _____ 36
Particleboard tile flooring installation _____ 34, 36
Partitions:
Adding _____ 59
Basement _____ 78
Changing _____ 17
Installing _____ 60
Nailing _____ 60
Relocating _____ 59
Removing _____ 59
Penetrating pigmented stain finishes:
Application _____ 81
Coats recommended _____ 81
Colors _____ 81
Cost _____ 81
Refinishing _____ 81
Plumbing:
Appraisal for rehabilitation _____ 10
Drainage system _____ 11
Fixtures _____ 11
Required additions _____ 11
Sewage disposal _____ 11
Water heater _____ 11
Water supply system _____ 10
Plywood and hardboard for interior finish:
Fastening _____ 63
Installation _____ 63
Nailing _____ 63
Sizes _____ 63
Stacking prior to installation _____ 64
Plywood panel siding:
Application _____ 36
Finishing _____ 36
Moisture content recommended _____ 26
Nailing _____ 36
Shiplap joints _____ 36
Sizes _____ 36
Porches:
Decay in _____ 5, 8
Floor _____ 72
Layout _____ 19
Posts _____ 72
Roof _____ 72
Steps _____ 71
Posts:
Basement _____ 4, 30
Porches _____ 72
Powder-post beetles _____ 9
Precautions when using chemicals for termite treatment _____ 30
Private area layout _____ 12, 16
Radiant heating _____ 11, 92
Reconditioning details _____ 83
Relaxation area layout _____ 13, 16
Resilient tile floors _____ 6
Roof coverings:
Wood shakes _____ 45

Page

Wood shingles _____ 44
Roof, wood-frame house:
Adding roof overhang _____ 42
Appraisal for rehabilitation _____ 6
Asphalt shingles _____ 6, 46
Coverings _____ 43
Decay in _____ 8
Flashing, appraisal for rehabilitation _____ 6
Flat _____ 58
Framing _____ 4, 41
Hip _____ 46, 58
Overhang _____ 6, 25, 42
Porch _____ 72
Repair _____ 42
Sheathing _____ 42
Ventilation _____ 58
Seamless flooring installation _____ 34
Sewage disposal _____ 11
Sheathing, roof _____ 42
Shed dormer:
Framing _____ 74
Size _____ 74
Sheet vinyl flooring installation _____ 34
Shingles:
Asphalt _____ 6, 46
Double-course application _____ 39
Single-course application _____ 39
Wood _____ 6, 44
Sidewall kitchen _____ 22
Siding and trim:
Application _____ 36
Appraisal for rehabilitation _____ 5
Bevel _____ 37
Decay in _____ 8
Hardboard siding _____ 37
Horizontal siding _____ 37
Masonry veneer _____ 41
Panel siding _____ 36
Plywood panel siding _____ 36
Vertical wood siding _____ 38
Wood shingle and shake siding _____ 39
Slab construction, protection from termites _____ 26
Softwood flooring _____ 33
Soil cover _____ 56, 89
Soil poisoning:
Basement houses _____ 30
Crawl-space houses _____ 26
Precautions when using _____ 30
Safety rules for _____ 30
Under slab construction _____ 26
Squeak elimination in floor framing _____ 31, 32
Steps, porches _____ 71
Sticking doors _____ 49
Storm windows _____ 5, 49, 54, 89
Strip flooring _____ 32, 33, 89
Subterranean termites _____ 9, 26, 89
Suspended ceiling _____ 64, 65, 78
Terminology _____ _inside back cover_
Termites:
Nonsubterranean termites _____ 9
Soil poisoning _____ 9, 26
Subterranean termites _____ 9, 26, 93
Tile, ceiling _____ 65
Traffic circulation in wood-frame structures _____ 12, 16, 17
Trim, cabinets and doors, appraisal for rehabilitation _____ 7
U-type kitchen _____ 22
Underlayments for wood flooring _____ 32
Uneven settlement of foundations _____ 1, 3, 30
Unfinished food (exterior) _____ 80
Utilities, construction required:
Bathtub framing _____ 70

Cutting floor joists --------------------------------- 69
Utility walls --------------------------------------- 70
Vapor barriers:
Blanket insulation with vapor barrier --------------- 56
Continuous membrane -------------------------------- 56
Installation --------------------------------------- 56
Location --------------------------------------- 10, 55
Materials --- 56
Purpose --------------------------------------- 10, 56
Soil cover -- 56
Vapor-resistant coating ------------------------ 10, 56
Veneers, masonry ------------------------------------ 41
Ventilation:
Attic and roof --------------------------- 10, 19, 57, 58
Cathedral ceilings --------------------------------- 58
Crawl space ------------------------------------ 56, 58
Flat roofs --- 58
Gable roofs -- 58
Hip roofs -- 58
Vertical wood siding:
Application -- 38
Nailing -- 38
Patterns --- 38
Wall framing:
Appraisal for rehabilitation ------------------------- 4
Patching involved when removing partitions --------- 59
Utility -- 79
Wall insulation:
Fill-type --- 54
Installing on masonry, brick, and stone walls ------- 55
Walls:
Basement --- 77
Finish --- 60, 77
Garage --- 79
Insulation ------------------------------------- 10, 54
Walls and ceilings:
Appraisal for rehabilitation -------------------------- 6
Interior covering ------------------------------------ 6
Painted surfaces ----------------------------------- 83
Trim, cabinets, and doors --------------------------- 7
Walls and piers, masonry and concrete --------------- 3
Wardrobe closets ------------------------------------ 69
Water heater -- 11
Water-repellent preservative finishes:
Application -- 80
Composition --------------------------------------- 80
Nails used on siding ------------------------------- 80

Water supply system --------------------------------- 10
Weathering of wood ----------------------------- 39, 80
Windows, wood-frame houses:
Appraisal for rehabilitation ------------------------- 5
Decay in -- 8
Functions -- 18
Placement --------------------------------------- 18, 47
Placement in remodeled kitchens -------------------- 23
Relocation --- 48
Repair of existing windows -------------------------- 47
Replacement of existing windows --------------------- 47
Storm windows ---------------------------------- 49, 54
Wood and fiberboard paneling for interior finish:
Nailing -- 64
Sizes -- 64
Stacking prior to installation ---------------------- 64
Wood-base tile flooring ----------------------------- 34
Wood block flooring --------------------------------- 34
Wood floor installation:
Base --- 32
Hardwood flooring ---------------------------------- 33
Installation over existing flooring ------------------ 32
Nailing -- 32
Softwood flooring ---------------------------------- 33
Strip flooring ------------------------------- 32, 33, 89
Underlayments -------------------------------------- 32
Wood block flooring --------------------------------- 34
Wood tile flooring ---------------------------------- 34
Wood-frame, structural:
Floor framing --------------------------------- 31, 32
Floor supports -------------------------------- 4, 31
Roof framing --------------------------------- 4, 41
Wall framing -- 4
Wood paneling, interior finish ---------------- 60, 64, 83
Wood piers -- 3
Wood properties and finish durability --------------- 80
Wood shakes for roofs ------------------------------- 45
Wood shingle and shake siding ----------------------- 39
Wood shingles for roofs:
Application -- 43
Appraisal for rehabilitation ------------------------- 6
Nailing -- 44
Species used --------------------------------------- 44
Wood tile --- 34
Work area, layout ------------------------------- 12, 16
Zoned living --------------------------------------- 16

ACKNOWLEDGMENTS

In the preparation of this handbook the author received much encouragement and many helpful suggestions from other staff members of the Forest Products Laboratory (FPL). I particularly wish to thank my associates in Wood Engineering Research, especially Billy Bohannan and J. A. Liska, for their assistance and suggestions in regard to the structural rehabilitation of buildings. The suggestions from other FPL scientists who are recognized authorities— W. E. Eslyn (pathology), G. R. Esenther (termites), and J. M. Black (finishes)—also added greatly to the breadth and completeness of this work.

I am also pleased to acknowledge the critique and help of Arthur M. McLeod, of Kaeser, McLeod, and Weston, Architect Engineer Associates, who did much to improve the practical utility of the handbook. I should also like to thank Theodore J. Brevik, professor of agricultural engineering at the University of Wisconsin, Madison, for his technical assistance.

Gerald E. Sherwood

The Forest Products Laboratory is maintained by the Forest Service, USDA, at Madison, Wis., in cooperation with the University of Wisconsin.